the cardboard box book

First published in the United States in 2006 by
Watson-Guptill Publications,
a division of VNU Business Media, Inc.
770 Broadway, New York, NY 10003
www.wgpub.com

Produced by Breslich & Foss Ltd, London
Designed by Balley Design Associates
Photographs by Martin Norris
Illustrations by Josh Halloran

Library of Congress Control Number: 2005935223

ISBN 0-8230-0610-7

Printed and bound in China

First Printing, 2006

1 2 3 4 5 6 7 8 / 12 11 10 09 08 07 06

the cardboard box book

25 things to make and do with empty boxes ✂

by Danny, Jake, and Niall Walsh

Watson-Guptill Publications
New York

Contents

Introduction

Fun is the object of this book: having lots of fun, stimulating the imagination, and spending very little money. Getting crafty with cardboard boxes is also an ideal way to keep dad amused on dull, rainy days.

Your cardboard creations can be painted and decorated with whatever you have on hand. The only limit to your experiments will be your imagination, bedtime, or your mother's realization that you've used her best saucepans as radio transmitters in your latest space probe.

At the top of each project you'll find three bits of key information. The first, "Time," tells you roughly how long it will take you to complete the project as shown in the photographs. (On pages 10–11 there's a list of how quickly each project can be made if you cut out the painting and decorating part.) The second bit of information, "Parental stress factor," is a rough guide to the amount of anxiety the project is likely to cause to the average parent. The third, "Fiddly bits," warns you about any tricky parts of the project.

If a project must have complicated instructions, then it becomes, well, not much fun! So all we've given you is a few diagrams and some basic instructions to get you started—we hope you'll discover your own methods and tricks. Good luck!

Niall Walsh   *Jake Walsh*   *Danny*

Parental stress factor

Here's how to read the ratings:

❶ No problem. The parent remains completely calm. All is well with the world.

❷ This indicates a noticeable increase in anxiety levels, way out of proportion to the actual level of disruption causing it. This exaggerated reaction will subside fairly quickly. Do nothing. Often, the parent will be speechless at this stage.

❸ Skilled intervention is required, or else you will reach scary Factor 4. The parent has rediscovered his or her power of speech and has turned up the volume. Remain calm, so as not to antagonize the parent. Apologize profusely, make your eyes go wide, and smile charmingly. This is usually enough to defuse the situation. Wait five minutes and continue as if nothing has happened.

❹ This is serious and if this level is reached you should stop working immediately. The parent has lost all grip on reality and is beyond rational argument. Remove yourself from the situation, save what you can, and regroup when the dust has settled.

Sensible Stuff

This is the boring bit, but please read it. That way, you'll have all the materials you need and you'll avoid causing serious damage to yourself and your home.

Cardboard boxes

All the projects in this book are made from cardboard boxes or sheets of cardboard cut from boxes. Supermarkets are usually happy to give away small and medium cardboard boxes. Furniture warehouses and stores selling big stuff like refrigerators might give you really huge boxes if you ask nicely. So that you don't end up cluttering your house, open up the seams and store your boxes flat.

Boxes come in many different shapes and sizes. These are the sizes we use the most:
- small cardboard boxes, about 10 in. x 10 in. x 10 in. (25 cm x 25 cm x 25 cm)
- medium cardboard boxes, about 12 in. x 12 in. x 18 in. (30 cm x 30 cm x 45 cm)
- large cardboard boxes, about 2 ft. x 2 ft. x 3 ft. (60 cm x 60 cm x 90 cm)
- cereal boxes
- shoe boxes
- stacking fruit boxes
- medium cardboard, about ⅛ in. (3 mm)
- thick cardboard, about ¼ in. (7 mm)

Basic tool kit
These are the things you will need for most projects:
- pencils
- ballpoint pens
- markers
- water-based poster paints
- assorted paintbrushes
- masking tape (lots)
- craft glue
- PVA glue and small brush
- craft knife
- scissors
- ruler

Paint and Glitter
When using paint, glitter, and other great, messy stuff, keep these things in mind:
- Cover tables and work surfaces with newspaper before painting or adding glitter to your creations.
- Wear an old shirt over your clothes to keep them clean.
- Always rinse paintbrushes thoroughly with cold water before putting them away so they will be ready the next time you need them.

Sticky stuff

• Water-based hobby glue can be used for gluing large surfaces and is good on thin cardboard and paper. To stick things like pebbles and twigs together, we've suggested you use PVA glue, which is stronger.

• Masking tape is stronger and easier to paint over than clear office tape. It comes in different widths, and you'll need lots of it.

Take care!

• Very large boxes often have stapled edges. Be careful when taking out the staples so you don't get scratched.

• You can use closed scissors to make a hole in cardboard, but never put your hand under the hole you are making.

• If you are using a craft knife to cut a sheet of cardboard, do it on a cutting board—not on the dining-room table or your bedroom carpet!

• If in doubt about anything, ask an adult for help. It makes them feel important.

Tip: Use the back, blunt edge of a knife to score along ruled lines before folding them. This will give you a nice, clean edge.

How to use templates:

In this book, we've given you templates for some of the projects. To use them, photocopy the page from the book, increasing the template in size if you need to. Cut out the paper pattern you have made, lay it on your sheet of cardboard, and draw around the pattern with a pencil. Cut around the line and you'll have your cardboard shape!

How to Add Light

Impress all your friends by adding electric light to your projects! It's easy to do and all the pieces you need are available from hardware stores. The amount of wire needed depends on what you are illuminating. To give you an idea, you'll need about 3 ft. (90 cm) of wire for the Christmas Diorama (page 82) or the Aquarium (page 48).

You will need:
- 1 battery holder
- 2 1.5-volt batteries (AA size)
- 2 bulb holders
- 2 2.5-volt bulbs with screw fittings
- small switch
- length of insulating wire about 3 ft. (90 cm) long
- masking tape

Here's what you do:
1 Place the batteries in the battery holder, making sure you put them in the right way around. (Place the + on each battery next to the positive sign on the holder.)
2 Attach a wire between the battery holder and the switch.
3 Wire the switch to one of the bulb holders.
4 Wire this bulb holder to the next bulb holder.
5 Wire the second bulb holder to the other terminal of the battery holder.
6 Make two holes in your cardboard creation, and poke the bulbs through. Tape the bulb holders and the battery holder to the back of the box and switch on.

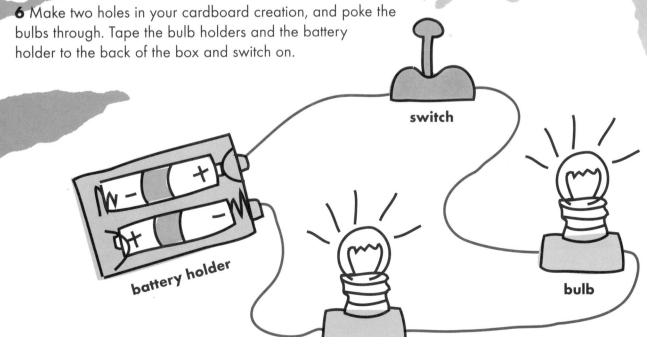

switch

battery holder

bulb

bulb

How Much Time Do You Have?

Some of the projects in the book take much longer to make than others. To help you figure out what you have time for, we have divided them up into three categories: projects that can be done in an hour or so, some that might take up a morning or an afternoon, and a few that will keep you busy for days on end! Don't be put off if we say a project takes a few hours to make—lots of time is taken up just waiting for paint or glue to dry.

If you're short on time, you can sometimes skip the painting and decorating stages, but it's usually worth spending a while longer and adding some color and sparkle to your creations. Some projects, such as the **Bus Photograph Frame** (page 16), would be really dull if you didn't decorate them, so we haven't given you an undecorated time for these. Check out the lists below for how long the decorated and undecorated projects might take to make.

Up to one hour

	Decorated	Undecorated
Bus Photograph Frame, page 16	An hour or less	–
Trail Stick, page 24	As long as the walk takes	–
Insect Box and Bug Catcher, page 98	About an hour	–
Guessing Box, page 112	About an hour	Half an hour

One to three hours

	Decorated	Undecorated
Ring Toss, page 12	A couple of hours	About an hour
Blow Soccer, page 22	A couple of hours	Under an hour
Drum Kit, page 26	About three hours	About an hour

	Decorated	Undecorated
Airplanes, page 32	A couple of hours per plane	About an hour
Potato Bowling, page 38	About an hour	Half an hour
Action Hero Tepee, page 54	A couple of hours	Under an hour (with no camp fire)
Mini Rockets, page 60	A couple of hours	Half an hour
Indoor Den, page 64	About three hours	About an hour
Dinosaurs, page 66	About an hour per dinosaur	Under an hour
Fishing Game, page 72	A couple of hours	About an hour
Christmas Diorama, page 82	About three hours	–
Climbing Wall, page 88	A couple of hours	About an hour
Wall Window, page 102	A couple of hours	–

More time than sense

	Decorated	Undecorated
Horse Racing, page 18	Days	–
Shield and Sword, page 28	Several hours for the shield (because of the papier-mâché). Under an hour for the sword.	–
Zoo, page 42	Days	–
Aquarium, page 48	About a day	–
Road Layout, page 76	Several hours to several days	Half an hour (if you just draw in the roads)
Play House, page 92	Days	A couple of hours
Space Rocket, page 106	Days	Several hours

Ring Toss

This is an aiming game of considerable skill that is easy to make and guarantees fun at parties and play dates.

Time: A couple of hours of work will give you a game that looks good and will last.

Parental stress factor: ❷ Parents will enjoy trying to beat you but, as things are being thrown, they will probably get nervous. Soon you will hear the familiar sounds of, "Be careful!," "That was close!," and "Shouldn't we move this outside?"

Fiddly bits: None.

You will need

- 2 garden stakes, about 18 in. (45 cm) in length
- 2 garden stakes, about 12 in. (30 cm) in length
- 2 fruit boxes
- craft glue
- masking tape
- 1 cardboard tube
- thin cardboard
- scissors or craft knife
- 4 garden stakes, about 10 in. (25 cm) in length
- number stickers
- thick cardboard (for the rings)
- fluorescent contact paper

1 Make the target poles

Take the four tallest garden stakes and wedge one into each corner of a fruit box, making sure that stakes of the same height are diagonally across from each other. Glue and tape them in place.

2 Create the pillar

Cut a circular base a couple of inches wider than the diameter of the cardboard tube in the piece of thin cardboard. Cut a hole in the center of the base the same size as the roll. Tape the roll upright onto the base, then glue the whole thing onto the box floor in the center.

3 Cut the slots

About a quarter of the way along one of the long sides of the box, cut a slot to half way down. Make the slot the width of the cardboard of the second fruit box you will use. Repeat this on the other long side at the opposite end, in other words not right across from the first slot. You should end up with something like this:

4 Add more target poles

Cut the two short sides from the second box and make similar slots in both of them about a quarter of the way across the length. However, this time cut the slot from the bottom up. Wedge two of the shortest stakes to the ends of one of the short pieces and tape them in place like this:

5 Do it again

Wedge and tape the remaining two stakes to the ends of the other short piece. Slide them both into the slots you made in the first box in Step 3. You will now have a ring toss board with nine target poles. From above, the board should look something like this:

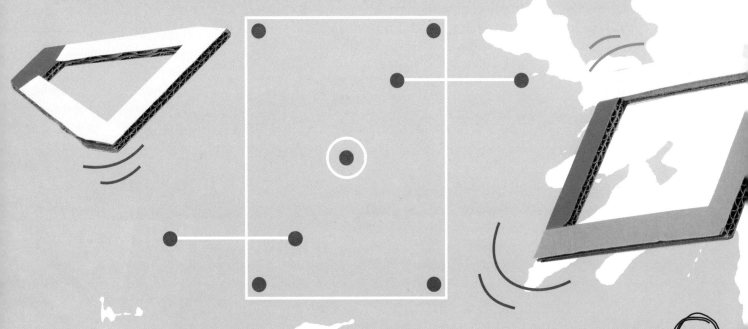

6 Score the poles

Give each pole a score according to how difficult you think each will be to hit. We printed out some score labels from the computer and stuck them next to each pole or on it. You could also use pre-printed stickers or draw your own.

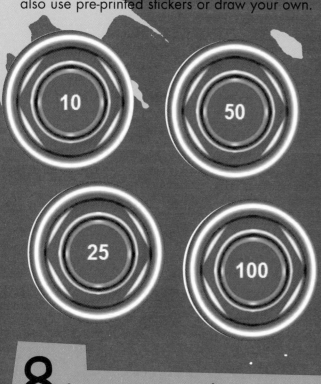

7 Make the rings

You need something to throw over the target poles. Cut hollow circles, triangles, and squares out of thick cardboard, making sure that these rings will fit over the poles.

8 Decorate the game

Cover the rings with pieces of fluorescent contact paper. We also added the same paper to the poles to make them stand out better.

How to play the game:

The object of the game is to throw the rings over the target poles that have the highest scores. Place the ring toss board on the floor and mark a throwing spot about 5 feet (1.5 meters) from it. Players should take turns to throw all three rings, one after another. Make a note of the first player's total score, then collect the rings and give them to the next player. You can have short games or long ones, going as many times as you like. The person with the highest score wins.

Variation:

Make a large version of the ring toss to play with outside. Glue four fruit boxes together into a square and glue or tape garden stakes wherever you want on the boxes. Color the ends of the stakes so they are easier to see and prop the whole thing up against a tree or wall so that it leans slightly. Stand way back and throw the rings. Suddenly it all seems a lot harder!

Bus Photograph Frame

If you thought photograph frames were boring, think again. The passengers in the bus windows are your friends.

Time: An hour or less depending upon how you decide to decorate the frame, plus paint- and glue-drying time.

Parental stress factor: ❶ Keep it low by including photographs of your parents, too.

Fiddly bits: Some tricky cutting out.

You will need

- 2 pieces thick cardboard, about 6 in. x 16 in. (15 cm x 40 cm)
- scissors or craft knife
- pencil and ruler
- assorted photographs
- PVA glue and small brush
- paint and paintbrush
- glitter, sequins, fun fur, etc., for decoration

1 Cut out the bus

Cut out a bus shape from some fairly thick cardboard. Design your own bus or copy the one shown below. Place your bus shape on top of another piece of cardboard, draw around it, and cut it out. You will now have a pair of buses that fit exactly over each other.

2 Make the windows

Count the photos you want to use. With the pencil and ruler, draw as many windows as you have photos onto one of your buses and carefully cut them out. This will be the frame and the other bus will be the backing.

3 Add the photos

Place the frame bus on top of the backing bus and draw around the inside of each window. One by one, place your photos in the windows. You may need to trim down your photos so they don't cover the ones next to them. Lay the frame bus over the images to check that you are showing the best part of the photo. Make any adjustments before gluing them down.

4 Color the frame

Paint the frame and let it dry. Then add glitter, sequins, fun fur—whatever you like. Decorate it how you want then just glue it onto the backing bus over the photos.

Variations:

• If you take lots of photographs or collect loads of stuff such as postcards, make a massive frame to use as a poster. Make a train shape and add carriages to it over time. Eventually the train could go all the way around your room!

• Make themed frames such as "My best friends," "My favorite places," "My favorite team," "My family," or "My vacation."

• Make a big Christmas bus with 25 windows as an alternative advent calendar. Remember to leave one side of each window uncut, so that it becomes a door to be opened.

Horse Racing

This is a racecourse on a large cardboard sheet with fences as jumps. Up to six people can play the game at one time.

Time: This could keep you busy for several days!

Parental stress factor: ❷ In the beginning, your parents may complain about the game's size. After that, any adults present are likely to try to take over this game. Be careful not to lose control of it.

Fiddly bits: None really.

You will need

- green and black paint and paintbrush
- thick cardboard, about 46 in. x 20 in. (120 cm x 50 cm)
- pencil
- black marker
- PVA glue and small brush
- aluminum foil
- wood, twigs, and gravel (for the fences)
- thin cardboard (for the cards)
- 1 dice
- 6 horse figures in different colors or styles (cowboys or soldiers will do)

1 Prepare the track

Paint the thick cardboard green. When the paint is dry, draw the race track onto the green area. The track is a large oval with a wavy trail across the middle, which will be a shortcut in the game. Draw the track and trail in pencil then go over them in black marker. If you want a parking lot, paint the area black.

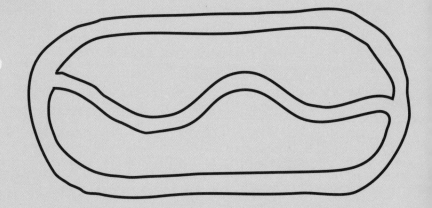

2 Draw in the spaces

Draw in the spaces on the track and along the shortcut with the black marker. We made the number of spaces in the shortcut 25 and the number in the outer track 26. This was sneaky. You decide how much of an advantage to give with your shortcut. In our version, players think they are gaining lots of spaces but they are not!

3 Add more detail

Add a finish line. In the square after this write "start," and mark the lines you want to be fences by making them thicker. Add a "C" in the center of the board. (This is where you put the cards you make in Step 5.) Write a "C" in squares around the track two or three spaces apart. Stick down aluminum foil for water jumps in two spaces and write "skip a turn" next to them.

4 Create the fences

Find some pieces of wood and cut them to size. The older and more worn the wood is the better, as it will look more real. You can also use twigs stuck together or some twigs on a bed of gravel. Don't be afraid to use lots of PVA glue because it will dry invisibly and will hold things together very well. When you have made your fences, glue them into place on the lines you drew in Step 3. To the right are some drawings of fences we made.

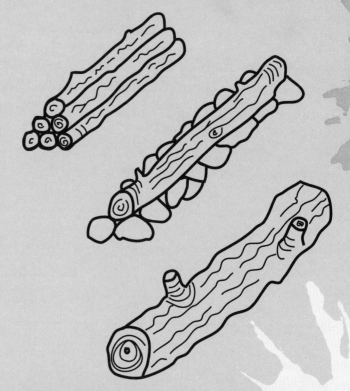

5 Make the cards

Cut the thin cardboard down into about 20 cards, each about 2 in. x 3 in. (5 cm x 7.5 cm). You decide what to write on the cards but, beware! You might land on those squares and have to do as the card says.

Things we wrote on our cards:
- Horse in front falls, have another turn.
- Get boxed in, skip a turn.
- Horse trips, skip a turn.
- Fall off your horse, go back three spaces.
- Horse hits the fence, go back one space.
- Dog bites horse on bottom, move ahead three spaces.
- Horse throws you, go back two spaces.

How to play the game:

• You need some horse figures to use as the players' pieces and a dice. Each player throws the dice once and the one with the highest score starts. The player to his or her left goes next.

• Each player throws the dice and moves his or her horse forward the number of spaces on the dice, but feel free to make up your own rules. For example, we decided that you should get another turn if you threw a one.

• You can only access the shortcut if you end a move on the square next to the beginning of the shortcut.

• If you land on a "C," you must take a card and do as it says, then place it back at the bottom of the pile.

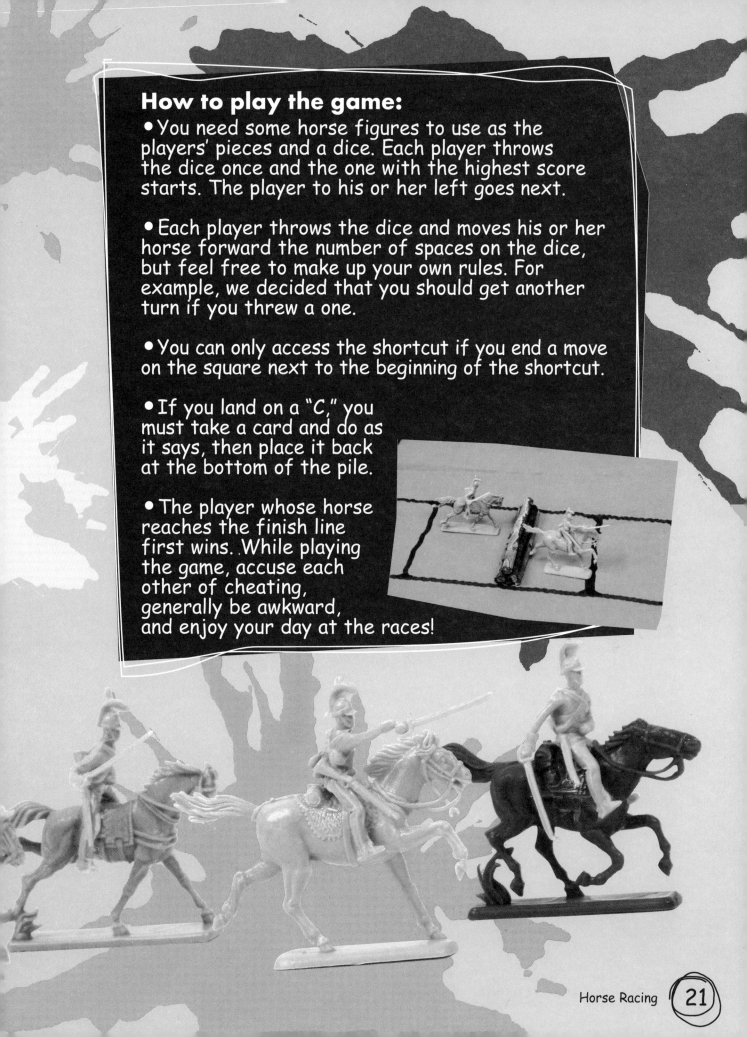

• The player whose horse reaches the finish line first wins. While playing the game, accuse each other of cheating, generally be awkward, and enjoy your day at the races!

Blow Soccer

The basic game is quick to make and great fun to play. Absolutely no skill is required unless you win, in which case claim it was all due to your cleverness.

Time: The basic game can be put together in less than an hour if you don't decorate it. Otherwise, allow a couple of hours for the paint to dry.

Parental stress factor: ❸ Caution! The sight of you drooling from the end of a straw, along with the possibility of crowd trouble and head injury, could raise parental stress a bit, so this gets a mid to high rating.

Fiddly bits: None.

You will need

- disposable cardboard box
- stacking fruit box
- scissors or craft knife
- green paint and paintbrush
- pencil and ruler
- black marker
- old comics or magazines
- craft glue
- ping-pong ball
- 1 straw per player
- clear varnish (optional)

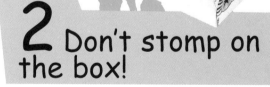

1 Stomp on the box!

Take a cardboard box, place it on the ground, and jump up and down on it, shouting "Blow soccer!" until the box is a crumpled heap. Having done this, you will be ready to embark on the project, chilled, relaxed, and at one with the world.

2 Don't stomp on the box!

Take your fruit box—it's okay, we're really going to make something this time. Cut a goal at each narrow end, like this:

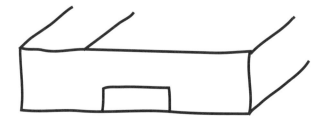

3 Paint the field

Paint the inside bottom of the box green and let it dry. Mark out a soccer field with your pencil and ruler, then go over the lines in black marker. This is what the markings should look like:

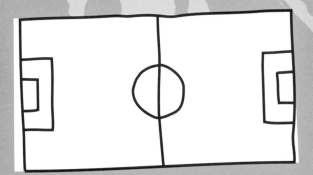

4 Decorate the box

Cut figures from comics or magazines and paste them around the inside of the box. Our soccer stadium features some terrible drawings—the sillier the better.

Tip: If you want to make it harder to score, cut a small hole above each goal and push extra straws through these holes. This will also ensure that foreheads don't crash into each other in the heat of the game.

How to play the game:

• Take turns to drop the ping-pong ball into the center circle, then each player should blow like crazy through his or her straw until a goal is scored. Repeat until halftime, then repeat until the end of the game. (This is quite tiring, so five minutes for each half is usually more than enough.)

• Players must not touch the box at any point during the game. This is easier said than done, as it is only natural to want to give the ball a helping hand.

• An opponent might lean right over the field and blow from in front of your goal. This, of course, is a foul and a tactic you would never use.

• After a couple of minutes of frantic blowing, lots of spit will dribble from the ends of the straws. While this lends a certain amount of realism to the game (think of playing conditions on a rainy day), it also makes the ball stop and the paint run. A good remedy is to varnish the field, which allows you to wipe the surface clean as necessary. If this seems like too much work, rename the game water polo and carry on.

Trail Stick

This is brilliant. It has absolutely nothing to do with cardboard boxes, but is too good not to tell you about. I suppose we could say that you should keep it in a cardboard box—in fact, you must! Problem solved.

Time: As long as a walk takes.

Parental stress factor: ❶ Adults being adults, they will find something to complain about. In this case it may well be the objects you choose to decorate your stick. For example, if you're lucky enough to find a dead squirrel's tail, you should probably think twice about taking it home.

Fiddly bits: None, other than getting rubber bands over rough sticks without snapping them.

You will need

- rubber bands
- strong stick, about 2 feet (60 cm) long
- parents who go on walks
- cardboard box

1 Find cool stuff

Next time you're on a walk, collect anything that catches your fancy and will remind you of where you went. Attach everything to the stick with rubber bands.

2 Put your trail stick in the box!

When you get home, carefully place your trail stick in a cardboard box.

Reality check:
North American Indians used to keep a record of their journeys by collecting bits and pieces along the way. They attached these reminders to a stick as they went along. They could then tell other tribe members how to make the same journey by showing them the trail stick.

Drum Kit

Cardboard is not normally valued for its musical qualities, so prepare to be amazed by the variety of sounds that come out of it. The other bonus is the well-known therapeutic benefit that comes from spending a couple of hours making something, then smashing it to pieces.

Time: An hour's work will give you a simple, undecorated version. Allow longer if you decided to paint and decorate it.

Parental stress factor: ❹ Your parents will either marvel at your inventiveness and skill at making a musical instrument from such primitive materials or recoil in horror as they witness its frenzied destruction.

Fiddly bits: None whatsoever.

You will need

- 8 to 12 cardboard boxes of varying sizes
- stool or small chair
- masking tape
- PVA glue and small brush
- plastic bottles and tin cans
- pieces of thick cardboard and cardboard tubes
- garden stakes or sticks
- assorted paints and paintbrush (optional)
- colored paper and aluminum foil (optional)
- drum sticks (or a pair of sturdy sticks)

1 Assemble your boxes

The aim is to put together a collection of boxes around a stool. Use big boxes as a base upon which to fix other, smaller boxes. Use as much tape and glue as necessary to stick everything together securely—your drum kit should last for at least ten minutes.

2 Add other elements

Add other used containers, such as plastic bottles, margarine tubs, or tin cans, as these will add to the variety of sound. Tape garden stakes or sticks to the boxes then place the bottles and cans upside down on them. Stick cardboard tubes in any handle spaces and place pieces of thick cardboard on the top surfaces of your creation.

3 Paint your drum kit

If you are feeling artistic, paint circles onto the thick pieces of cardboard on the top surfaces to indicate where they should be hit to achieve the best sound. Then go ahead and paint the sides and decorate the drums with colored paper, aluminum foil, etc. Do bear in mind, though, that your drum kit is being built to be destroyed!

4 Perform!

Buy the cheapest pair of drum sticks you can or make some out of sturdy sticks. Sit down on the stool and admire your creation. Ideally it will be an unrecognizable mass of cardboard, tape, bits of plastic, and tin that you won't mind destroying. Breathe deeply and feel at one with it. Now you need to think about what to play. What is the best piece of drumming you have ever heard? Select the track, play it through headphones, turn it up very loud, and smash the drum kit to pieces!

5 Deal with the mess

After the gig, you'd better clean up everything as soon as possible or we cannot be held responsible for the parental stress factor going off the scale—that's if mom and dad haven't already had a meltdown by the performance.

Shield and Sword

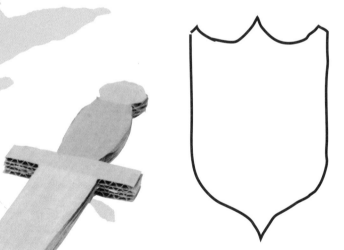

Personalize a shield to represent you and your family. The idea can also be adapted to make coats of arms and flags.

Time: Our superior shield for high-ranking knights requires a few hours of glue- and paint-drying time.
Parental stress factor: ❷ This depends on how you deal with the messy papier-mâché stage.
Fiddly bits: None. (Well, kind of nearly none.)

You will need

- pencil and ruler
- 2 sheets thick cardboard, about 20 in. x 15 in. (50 cm x 38 cm)
- scissors or craft knife
- PVA glue and small brush
- jar
- white paper towels
- red, black, gold, and silver paint and paintbrush
- masking tape

1 Cut out your shield

Draw this basic shield shape on a single piece of thick cardboard.

Tip: If you were a knight, planning to use the shield in battle, you would need some very thick cardboard. In fact, you would be better off with wood or steel. However, since this shield is more for show than battle, cardboard will do, but make it thick, just in case you are attacked.

2 Add the cross piece and dividers

Cut a cross piece and upper and lower dividers out of the second piece of cardboard and stick them onto the shield to look like this:

3 Design your symbols

You must now decide what to put into each of the four quarters to represent you. What will it be? We chose a symbol of the city we live in, called the Lincoln Imp (you can look him up on the Web, but he is not a pretty sight), a tepee because we like camping, a bird because Danny likes bird-watching, and the sun because we all like vacations in hot places. Copy the shapes onto pieces of thick cardboard, cut them out, and glue them onto the four quarters of the shield. Here are our designs:

4 Give it strength

To strengthen the shield and give it an ancient look, cover it in papier-mâché. In a jar, mix up some PVA glue and water (1 part glue to 1 part water). Lay sheets of white paper towel all over the shield. Use an old paintbrush to slap the glue and water mixture onto the shield, making sure that the paper clings to the edges of the cardboard. Two layers should be sufficient to give the shield a nice robust feel. Let it dry.

5 Paint it

When the shield is totally dry, paint it. It is best to keep the design simple. Paint the cross one color then choose two different colors for the quarters. We think gold and silver paints add a medieval feel. Next, paint your figures. We chose black because it helps them stand out and makes your shield look bolder.

6 Make a hand grip

To be able to hold your shield the way knights did, you need to attach a hand grip to the back. Cut a strip of cardboard 2 in. (5 cm) wide and 1 foot (30 cm) long. Grab this piece of cardboard in the middle and place the back of your clenched fist on the back of the shield where you want the hand grip to be. Still holding the cardboard, bend the rest of it down around your fist and flatten it out onto the shield. Glue it down in this position to make your hand grip. Using the papier-mâché technique mentioned in Step 4, glue two layers of paper towel over the ends of the hand grip to strengthen it, and it will give you a lifetime of service or your money back.*

7 Finally, create the sword

For a robust sword, cut two identical sword shapes out of thick cardboard and glue them together with PVA glue. When it has dried, paint your sword gold and silver.

The Cardboard Box Book

Variations:

If you enjoyed making the shield, you might like to try a coat of arms or a flag.

Coat of arms

A shield that has a motto on the front, but no hand grip is called a coat of arms. Follow Steps 1 to 5 of the shield project, but leave space for a motto. Cut out a piece of cardboard in the shape of a scroll. Write your motto on it (or just your family name), and glue it to the top of your coat of arms. If you glue some string to the back, you'll be able to hang it on the wall. This is an opportunity to check out your family history and discover whether you are descended from pirates or criminals. You can do this on the Internet or at a good library. You may discover that you have a family crest, and then you will feel that you are better than the rest of us. We Walshes have a rather nice coat of arms, but our motto is "Transfixus sed non mortuus," which, we are told, means "Killed, but not dead!"

You can also decorate the coat of arms with family photographs and pictures from magazines showing your favorite things. Stick the motto on the top and you have a unique scrapbooked family coat of arms!

Flag

Using design ideas from the shield and the coat of arms, make a flag. There is no need to sew it, just cut out the designs from bits of cloth and stick them onto a larger background piece with fabric glue. Whenever we go camping we hang a skull and crossbones on the outside of the tent to let people know that we are available for choir practice and babysitting.

* Does not apply to hand grips made from brown or white cardboard, shields used in combat, shields produced after breakfast, and shields with hand grips on the back. This does not affect your statutory rights.

Airplanes

These planes are very big, and very flyable. There is plenty of room for experimentation and you can have fun inventing flashy designs and names for your aircraft.

Time: An hour will produce a rather splendid and enormous plane. Allow extra time for the glue and paint to dry.

Parental stress factor: ❶ As long as you let dad test your plane first, this will be a low-stress project. It's a boy thing and he'll never grow out of it.

Fiddly bits: Some aerodynamic modifications may be required depending on the coefficient of the velocitude to body mass index of the wing surface area, given the prevailing wind conditions at the time of flight.

You will need (for each plane)

- medium cardboard, about 3½ feet x 2 feet (1 meter x 60 cm)
- pencil and ruler
- PVA glue and small brush
- paperclips
- craft knife
- assorted paints and paintbrush (for the Vulcan)
- silver spray paint (for the Silver Scorcher)
- airforce stickers

1 Choose your model

Select the airplane you'd like to make from page 37.

2 Score and fold your cardboard

Score and fold the sheet of cardboard in half down the middle of its longest side, then use your pencil and ruler to mark a line parallel to the center fold about 1 in. (2.5 cm) from it. Repeat on the other side of the fold. Score and fold both of these lines. You should end up with something that from the top looks like this:

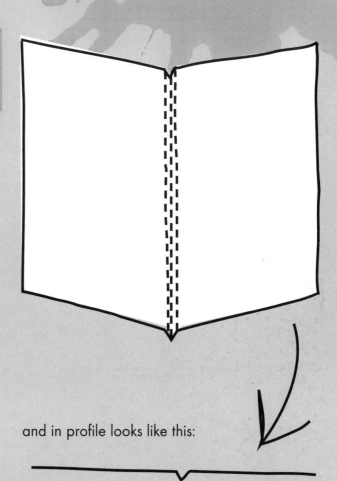

and in profile looks like this:

3 Glue it together

Now glue the two 1 in. (2.5 cm) sides together to form the fuselage. Clamp them together with paperclips until the glue is dry.

4 Draw the wings

With the two sides folded together, mark your wing shape, according to the model you have chosen.

VULCAN

SILVER SCORCHER

BIRD

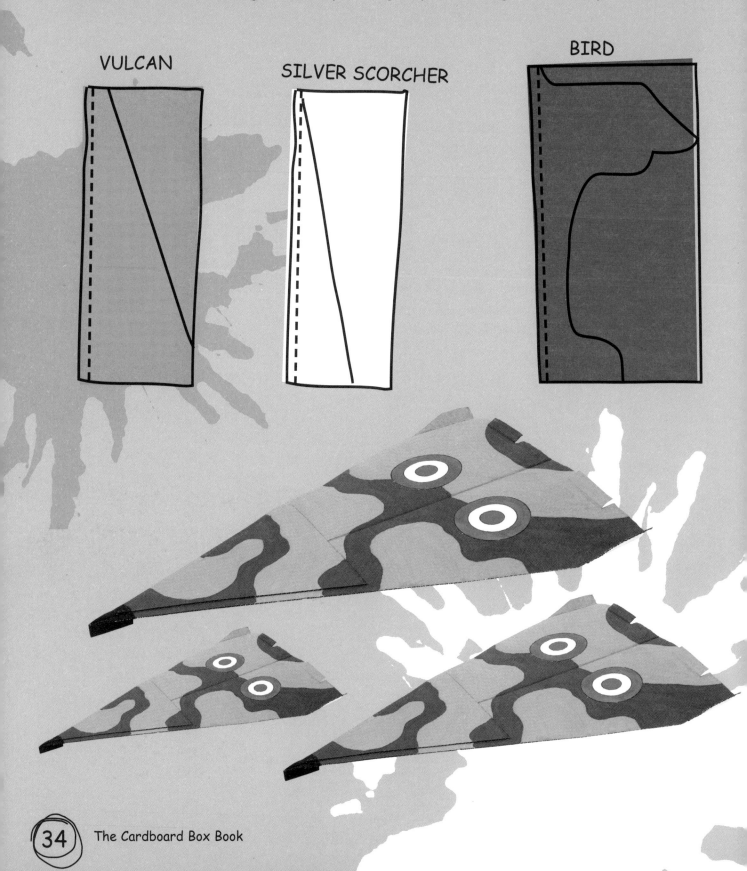

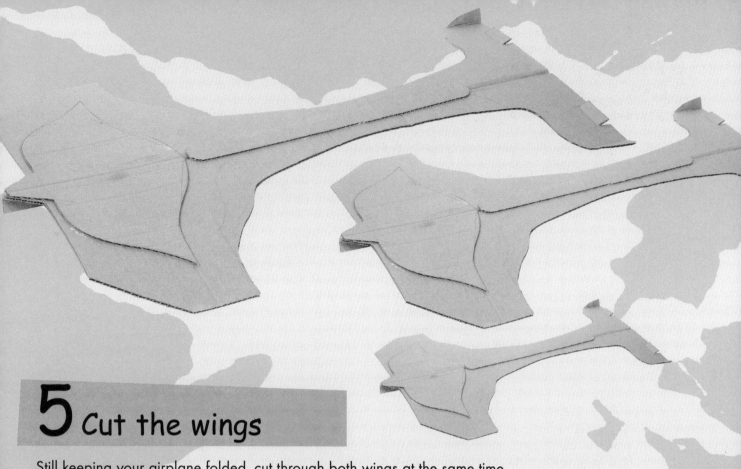

5 Cut the wings

Still keeping your airplane folded, cut through both wings at the same time with a craft knife. Open the wings back up and cut out small triangular or shaped pieces of cardboard depending on your model. Glue these to the front topside to add extra weight, strengthen the plane, and help it fly further.

VULCAN   SILVER SCORCHER   BIRD

6 Make the flaps

Now follow the cut (solid) and fold (dashed) lines in the illustrations in Step 5 for your chosen model to add flaps. Turn up the edges of the wing tips. In profile, the planes should look like this:

VULCAN

SILVER SCORCHER

BIRD

7 Fly it right now or paint it

Your plane will be flyable now if you can't wait to test it. Otherwise, paint it following our suggestions, or exactly as you wish. We decorated two of our planes with air force symbols printed from the computer and some of those weird numbers you get on planes. Our Bird was an experiment in aviation techniques, which we left undecorated. When your plane is dry, you might have to press the wings flat by placing some heavy books on them: paint can make them warp and bend a little.

Choose a model:

Here are three different planes to try.

Vulcan

To make the Vulcan, paint the underside white or pale blue and the top in camouflage colors. The idea is that from beneath your plane will be hard to see against the sky; from above, the enemy won't be able to spot it, as it will blend in with the vegetation on the ground.

Silver Scorcher

This is similar in shape to the Vulcan, but much sleeker. You may need to experiment with weight at the nose by taping some coins or washers up front to get the balance just right, but when you do, you'll see why it's called the Silver Scorcher. To decorate, take it outside and spray it with a can of silver paint. Make sure you don't spray with the wind against you unless you want a new hair color or silver jeans. Spray the paint with quick, even motions otherwise it might become too thick and run.

Bird

This shape will bring out the engineer in you. It will not fly brilliantly at first, but this is deliberate. You must work out how to adjust it to make it sail through the air. You might need more weight up front or more wing area. We strengthened our Bird with a fancy shape on its back and a straight piece along the spine of the fuselage. Sooner or later yours will fly. Good luck!

Potato Bowling

This is a totally fun and unpredictable potato-rolling game with the option of becoming a coin-tossing game as well.

Time: About an hour to make and paint it. A quick, no-frills, undecorated version can be made in half an hour.

Parental stress factor: ❷ You might raise a few eyebrows as you ask for some potatoes to use for target practice. Some parents think potatoes are food, not toys.

Fiddly bits: It takes a certain skill to direct a nubby potato.

You will need

- 3 potatoes
- scissors or craft knife
- medium-sized cardboard box
- assorted paints and paintbrush
- black marker
- small cardboard box (for the coin-tossing game and the variation)
- coins
- PVA glue and small brush
- candy (and lots of it!)

1 Select your spuds

It is best if your three potatoes are slightly oddly shaped, as this will make their paths unpredictable and the game more exciting. Using the potatoes as a guide to size, cut three irregular shapes out of one side of the box, each a different width.

2 Paint and score the box

Paint the whole box in bright colors and let it dry. Allocate scores to the holes, such as 10 for the biggest hole, 20 for the medium, and 50 for the smallest. Write the numbers in black marker above the holes.

3 Add a second target

To incorporate a coin-tossing game into the box, decide what size coin you are going to use and cut a hole in the center of the top of the box twice the diameter of the coin. This is your target.

4 Make the back shield

Hitting the target with a coin from a distance is quite difficult, so add a back shield to prevent coins from rolling away and getting lost. Cut a small box in half diagonally. (Keep the other half for the variation described on page 41.) Cut away one of the remaining square sides, leaving just enough edge to fold out and glue down onto the big box. Paint the back shield and let it dry.

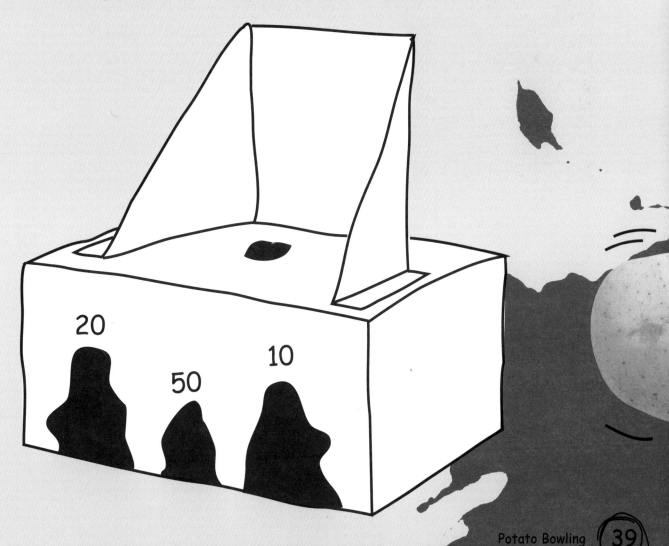

How to play the games:

Here are our rules for potato bowling and coin-toss.

Potato bowling
Place the box on the ground and mark the spot from which to roll your potatoes: about 9 feet (3 meters) is a good distance. The potatoes have to go right through the holes to score. It is interesting the way a perfectly bowled potato can suddenly change direction at the last minute.

Coin-toss
Take a handful of coins and again stand at the mark. Try to throw the coins into the hole in the box top. This is not as easy as it sounds and can become quite addictive.

Variation:

This variation makes use of the leftover half of the small box used in Step 4. Cut six small, shaped holes into one of the sloping sides and decorate the box however you want. If you are getting bored of painting, try some decoupage—a French name for sticking lots of pictures all over something.

Mark a throwing line some distance away and aim small candies at the holes. Those that go through the holes in the box you can eat! So the better your aim, the less likely you are to need any dinner.

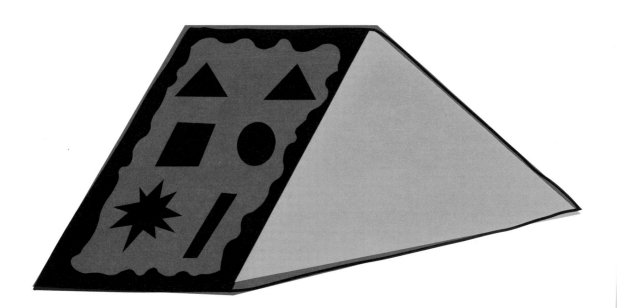

Zoo

This is a large play base with various animal enclosures. It is a project you can add to and take pride in.

Time: You could happily spend several weekends on this: it all depends on how realistic you want your penguin pool to be. The base can be made quickly, but creating and painting the enclosures will add time.

Parental stress factor: ❷ The zoo is not likely to cause any serious traumas, but size is always a potential problem with parents.

Fiddly bits: Making the cardboard fences is easy, but quite a lot of messy gluing is involved.

You will need

- 3 fruit boxes
- scissors or craft knife
- PVA glue and small brush
- masking tape
- 2 large sheets of cardboard, about 30 in. x 14 in. (76 cm x 36 cm), to support the base and make the entrance
- assorted paints and paintbrush
- several smaller sheets of medium cardboard (for the enclosures)
- pencil and ruler
- piece of paper
- pins
- small amount of sand
- model grass
- aluminum foil
- small rocks, twigs, gravel, bamboo sticks, moss, lichen, grass (your choice, when you've decided on your animals)
- a selection of plastic animals

1 Make the base

Put the three fruit boxes together as shown below. Cut out sections from the walls to make two entryways between the boxes and one to the outside world, then glue the boxes together. When your base is dry, turn it over and tape a large sheet of cardboard to the underside.

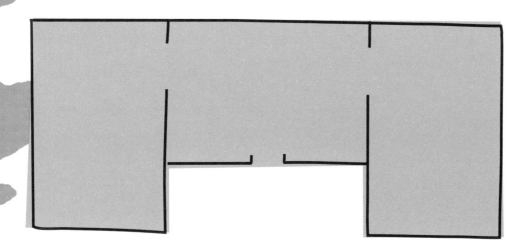

2 Create an entrance

Glue another piece of cardboard under the front section to form the driveway and parking lot. (The diagram will act as a source of great confusion as you try to understand this instruction.)

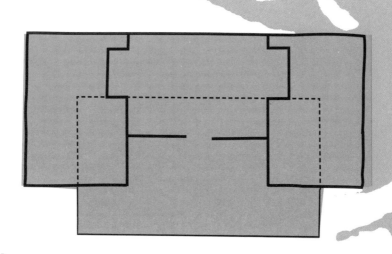

3 Paint the entrance

Paint the entry road and parking lot spaces brown and the rest of the entrance green to indicate grassy areas.

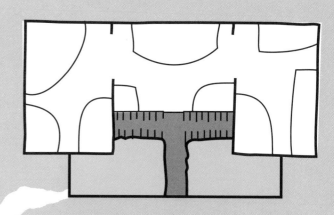

4 Design the inside of the zoo

Now it's time to decide where to put the enclosures. Draw a plan on a piece of paper and play around with various combinations and ideas until you are satisfied. You will probably alter your design as you build the layout, but it helps to have some sort of grand scheme in mind. The one we designed looked like the drawing above.

Reality check:

When you visit a zoo, try to find out about its conservation efforts (a fancy way of describing the things people do to protect animals in the wild). Today, conservation should be the main purpose of a zoo, rather than it being a place to satisfy our curiosity about how strange creatures behave. Such curiosity can be better satisfied at your local shopping mall on a Saturday morning or during feeding time at the local burger joint.

5 Make the enclosures

Make walls from strips of medium cardboard, about 1 in. (2.5 cm) wide, curved into the shape you want the enclosure to be. Hold the cardboard where you want the wall to go and draw along its edge onto the base. With a brush, glue along this pencil line, then stick the wall in place. To keep the wall in place while the glue dries, push pins through the cardboard and into the base.

> **Tip:** Cardboard walls can make up the bulk of the enclosures, but you can use twigs and sticks to make fences, or pebbles glued down in a row to make walls.

6 Create sandy areas

You need to re-create the correct habitats for your animals. Camels will need a sandy surface to make them feel at home in the desert. (Well, dromedary camels will, as they are desert dwellers, but bactrian camels feel at home on rough grass. Make sure you know which type you've got!) Rush off to the nearest beach, collect some sand, then paint the floor of a couple of cages with PVA glue and sprinkle sand over them.

7 Add leafy bits

Next let's turn our attention to the grazers, such as zebras and giraffes. You can just paint the floors of these areas green, but it's more fun to go to your local hobby shop and purchase a small quantity of model grass. This is fine sawdust painted green and it used by railway modelers. It's inexpensive and works perfectly for scaled-down plastic herbivores.

8 Introduce mud and water

Paint some of the enclosures plain brown for those animals, such as hippos, that like to wallow in mud. Glue down irregularly shaped pieces of aluminum foil to act as lakes, ponds, or pools to give your animals fresh water.

Tip: Small bits of gravel make useful borders for ponds, and sticks and twigs make effective scenery. Do not be afraid to glue down bits of dried up moss, lichen, and grass. These things will last and add that "natural" touch.

Bamboo cane split down the middle will make an impressive arch over the entrance, and you can also use it to line the sides of your entry road. Bamboo adds a nice jungle feel, too.

The Cardboard Box Book

9 Paint the outside

Use plenty of thick, green paint to create bush shapes over any offending writing on the outside of your fruit boxes. Before it has dried, add yellow and brown to vary the color of the foliage.

10 Add the animals

Now you are ready to receive your animals. Inexpensive, plastic wild animals can be found in most toy shops. Try to find some of the rarer animals like our favorite, the okapi. Check out its habitat needs and adapt one of your enclosures to make it feel right at home. As your zoo grows, just glue more boxes onto the sides and connect them by cutting through the wall.

Variations:

• Design a drive-through safari park with roads meandering through open areas full of lions, zebras, and wildebeest.

• Consider building a farm, instead of a zoo, complete with fields, mud, a duck pond, mud, buildings, barns, pig sties, more mud, stables, and, oh yeah, more mud.

Aquarium

This one is very impressive, believe me. Long lines will form outside your bedroom door. Let's waste no time.

Time: You could make this in a day, but it's nice to add to it gradually.
Parental stress factor: ❶ Parents will be delighted with your new fish-watching hobby.
Fiddly bits: A few parts require nimble fingers and the skilled use of scissors or a craft knife. Fixing up the lighting might also be a little tricky.

You will need

- medium-sized cardboard box
- masking tape
- silver spray paint or poster paint
- craft knife or scissors
- assorted paint and paintbrush
- glitter paint (optional)
- matchbox (for the treasure chest)
- aluminum foil
- green tissue paper
- scraps of green cloth
- PVA glue and small brush
- sand, twigs, and stones
- empty cereal box (for the fish)
- dark-colored thread

For the lighting (see page 9)

- 1 battery holder
- 2 1.5-volt batteries (AA size)
- 2 bulb holders
- 2 2.5-volt bulbs with screw fittings
- small switch
- insulating wire

1 Paint the outside

Seal the lid to the box with tape, then spray the box with silver paint. It's best to do this outdoors or let dad do it. It will make him feel important and any accidents—spills, large silver patches on the grass, or anything else likely to upset responsible adults—can be blamed on him. You can use silver poster paint instead, or paint it blue and green to match the inside of the tank. Allow the paint to dry.

2 Create a window

Cut a window in one long side of the box with the craft knife, leaving a border about 1 in. (2.5 cm) all the way around.

Tip: If you'd prefer something a little less abstract, cut out sea and water pictures from magazines and stick them to the walls inside your tank. (Paint the walls first.)

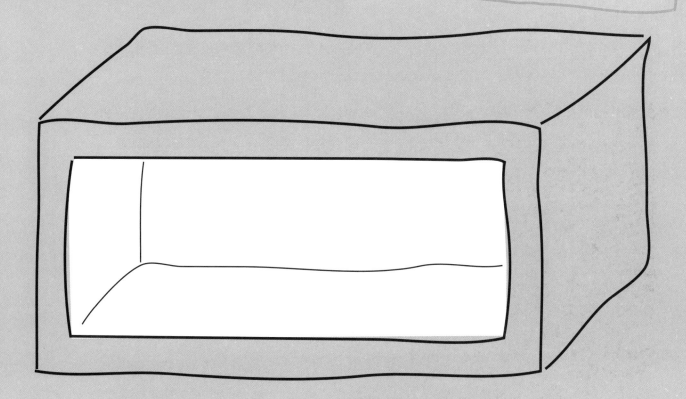

3 Paint the inside

Now decorate the inside of the box. First, paint the ceiling black, but leave the floor blank for now. When it has dried, paint the two sides and the back wall a swirly, watery blue and green. Let the paints run into each other and splash on some white and gray paint while the other colors are still wet. This creates a nice underwater look. You can enhance the effect by adding swirls of glitter paint. Let it dry.

4 Construct a treasure chest

Paint the matchbox brown and let it dry before adding some silvery touches. Slide the lid open and stuff aluminum foil inside to look like a stash of pirate silver. Or ask your mom if she has any diamonds or rubies she can lend you.

5 Add lots of seaweed

Create realistic-looking weeds for the ocean floor by twisting pieces of green tissue paper, coating them with glue, and leaving them to dry and harden. For dangly seaweed, cut "seaweedy" colored cloth into thin strips of various lengths, but not longer than the height of the aquarium. Hold a few strips next to each other and stick a piece of tape at the top to hold them together. Do several of these, then use more tape to stick them to the ceiling of the aquarium. Arrange them randomly, with some at the back and some at the front. (And don't forget to save some for the floor.) What you've got should now look something like this:

6 Make the seabed

Cover the bottom of the tank with glue, then pour sand all over it. A useful tip here is not to do this on the living room carpet, unless of course you're moving tomorrow. Tip the box gently from end to end to make sure that the base is completely covered with sand, but nice and lumpy. Scatter twigs and stones across the sand, add your treasure chest, and poke some more of the ocean weeds that you made in Step 5 into the sand so they look like they're sprouting from the seabed.

Tip: If you can't get ahold of sand, scrunched-up aluminum foil makes a great seabed. Wrinkled-up blue, green, brown, and sand-colored cloth looks okay, too.

7 Add the fish

Now you should be just about ready to make the fish. Use the fishy templates on the right to cut shapes out of cardboard and paint them. (See page 8 for instructions on drawing templates.) Remember to paint them on both sides: fish with "breakfast cereal" written along their sides tend to look unrealistic. When they are dry, attach the fish to pieces of dark-colored thread with small bits of tape and stick them to the ceiling of the tank with more tape.

Tip: Borrow a book on tropical fish from the library and photocopy them so that the tank contains pictures of realistic fish. Or you could get some fish-keeping leaflets from the local pet shop, cut out the fish pictures, and paste them to the back and sides of the tank.

8 Bring in the light

The simplest way to illuminate the tank is to make a hole in one corner and stick a small flashlight through it. Another idea is to rig up electric lights following the method given on page 9.

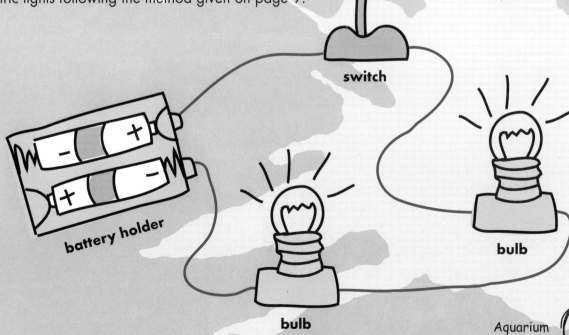

switch

bulb

battery holder

bulb

Action Hero Tepee

This tepee is just the right size for action figures to use as a camp.

Time: You can make the tepee and base in a couple of hours and do more work to it later if it fires your imagination.

Parental stress factor: ❶ There is nothing here to distress them.

Fiddly bits: Cutting the cardboard to shape is the hardest bit, but even that is pretty easy.

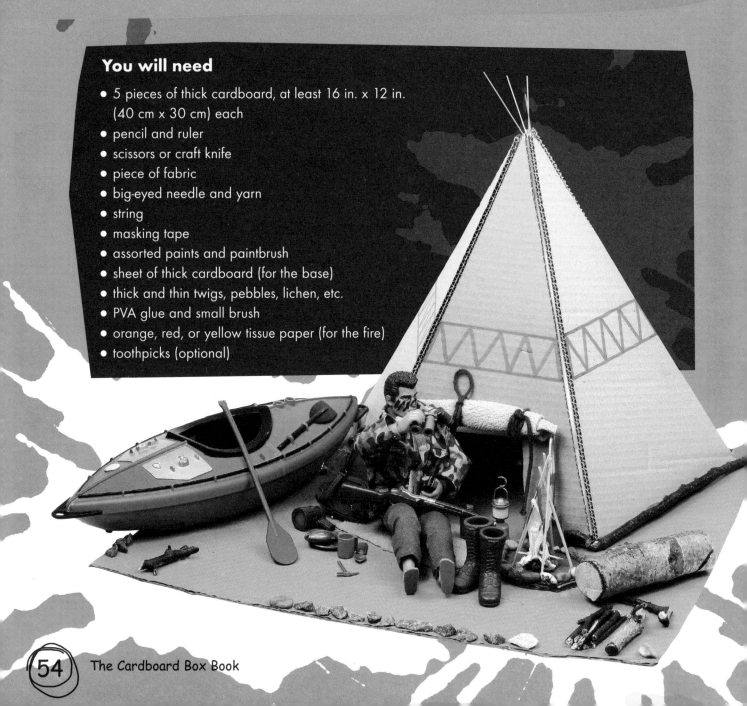

You will need

- 5 pieces of thick cardboard, at least 16 in. x 12 in. (40 cm x 30 cm) each
- pencil and ruler
- scissors or craft knife
- piece of fabric
- big-eyed needle and yarn
- string
- masking tape
- assorted paints and paintbrush
- sheet of thick cardboard (for the base)
- thick and thin twigs, pebbles, lichen, etc.
- PVA glue and small brush
- orange, red, or yellow tissue paper (for the fire)
- toothpicks (optional)

1 Cut the sides

The tepee has five sides that are exactly the same. Draw a line 9½ in. (24 cm) long along the shorter side of the first piece of cardboard. At the halfway point draw another line straight up at a right angle for 15 in. (38 cm). Draw two more lines from the top of this line to the ends of the 9½ in. (24 cm) line. You should now have a rather sharp pointed triangle like the one to the right. Draw and cut out five of these. You can also use the triangle at the right as a template if you want to make a larger or smaller tepee. (See page 8 for instructions on drawing templates.)

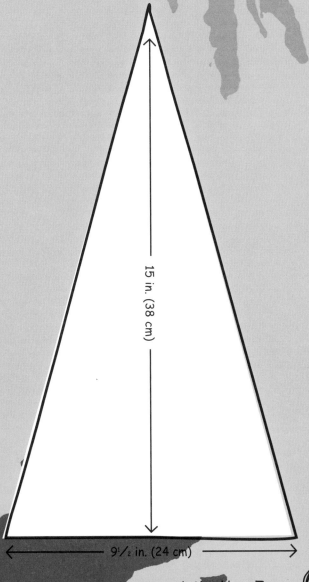

15 in. (38 cm)

9½ in. (24 cm)

Reality check:

In the interests of historical accuracy, we should mention that tepees were not originally constructed of cardboard. Tepees were clever tents built of frames of wooden poles covered with buffalo hides, and were the homes of Plains Indians, such as the Apache, Cheyenne, Comanche, and Sioux. The Indians hunted buffalo, following the herds, so they needed to get their tepees up and down quickly and easily. They could do this in a matter of minutes. Our tepee does not pretend to be an exact replica, but it does honor the skills of the Native Americans.

2 Construct the entrance flap

Cut out a door shape in one of the cardboard triangles. Place this piece of cardboard on the fabric and draw a line around it about ½ in. (1 cm) wider than the door. Cut this out and attach the cloth above the entrance by sewing through the cardboard.

Thread two pieces of yarn through the cardboard above the door and leave it hanging to the floor on the inside and outside. This will allow you to roll up the door curtain and tie it up when the tepee is finished. If you plan to paint your tepee (see Step 4), do that first before attaching the flap.

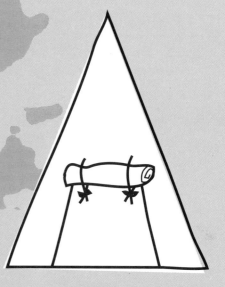

3 Get out the sticky tape

Place the five triangles together face down. Using fairly wide tape, attach each section to the next. (Do not tape the ends together to form the tepee shape yet.) This will leave you with a semicircle of cardboard. Turn it over and the outside of the tepee will be facing you.

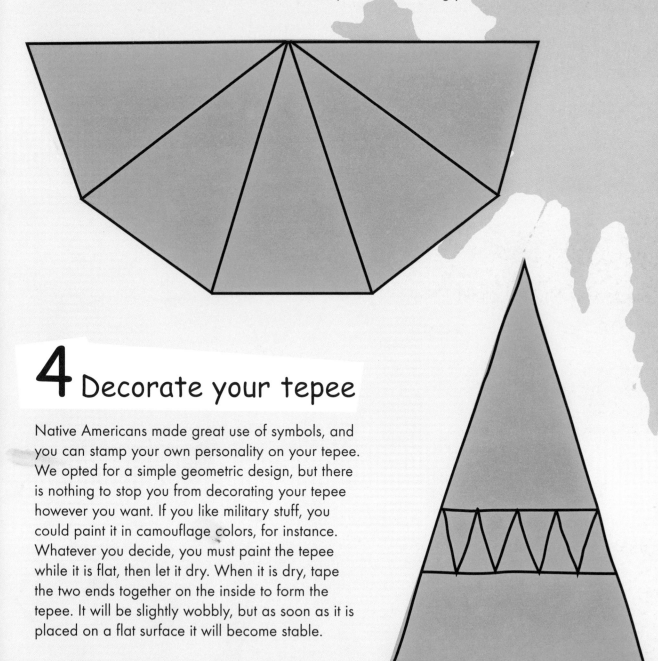

4 Decorate your tepee

Native Americans made great use of symbols, and you can stamp your own personality on your tepee. We opted for a simple geometric design, but there is nothing to stop you from decorating your tepee however you want. If you like military stuff, you could paint it in camouflage colors, for instance. Whatever you decide, you must paint the tepee while it is flat, then let it dry. When it is dry, tape the two ends together on the inside to form the tepee. It will be slightly wobbly, but as soon as it is placed on a flat surface it will become stable.

5 Create the base

Your tepee now needs a base. Select a large piece of thick cardboard and paint it green. While the paint is drying, go outside and look for twigs about ¼ in. (5 mm) thick. You also need to find a piece of a branch about 1 in. (2.5 cm) thick and 4 in. (10 cm) long. This will be your action hero's seat. You should also be on the lookout for pebbles, mosses, lichen, dead leaves, and rabbit poop. Authenticity is your aim.

6 Put it all together

Stick thin twigs around the edges of the base of your tepee with the PVA glue. Stick shorter pieces on either side of the door. Next, find five smaller twigs and stuff them into the top of the tepee, taping them into place on the inside. (Toothpicks can be used if you can't find twigs thin enough.) These represent the tops of the poles that form the frame of a real tepee. Stick the thickest twig outside the door so that our wilderness dude has something to sit on. Glue down the stones and bits of leaf, moss, and lichen.

7 Build a fire

A camp fire adds to the wilderness feel. Take a small piece of thick cardboard about 2½ in. x 2½ in. (6 cm x 6 cm) and cut it roughly into a circle. Squash small pieces of tissue paper into balls and glue them to the center of the cardboard circle to make embers. Twist long, thin pieces of tissue paper to look like flames and glue these to the embers. Glue thin twigs or toothpicks around the fire. Surround the fire with small stones and randomly place pieces of equipment outside the tent.

Variation:

If you have the time, you should consider wiring up the fire. Follow Step 7 above, but cut a hole for a bulb holder in the cardboard base and build your fire around this, hiding the bulb with the tissue paper. Connect the bulb to a battery holder following the instructions on page 9. Hide the batteries, wires, and switch inside or behind the tepee. Turn on the fire when night falls.

Mini Rockets

This is one of the best projects. With some clothing elastic and stiff cardboard you can make rockets that can be launched into the sky.

Time: Between half an hour and many hours, depending on how much you get into it and how detailed you want the rockets to be.

Parental stress factor: ❶ This gets a low rating unless you shoot off the rockets indoors, in which case the stress factor could go off the scale!

Fiddly bits: There is some semi-intricate cutting, which should be done by an adult—but supervise him or her at all times.

You will need

- pencil and ruler
- 2 sheets thick cardboard, about 20 in. x 6 in. (50 cm x 15 cm) per rocket
- length of thin clothing elastic, about 2 feet (60 cm) in length per player
- scissors or craft knife
- craft glue
- paint, aluminum foil, black marker, glitter (for decoration)

Tip: Experiment with the size and thickness of cardboard to get your rocket to go as fast as possible. The length of clothing elastic you need to make your rockets fly depends upon how strong it is, so do some tests and see what works best.

1 Draw and cut your rocket

Choose a rocket from the shapes to the right. Draw the rocket on the piece of cardboard and cut it out. (See page 8 for instructions on drawing templates.) The little notch near the top is where you will put the elastic before stretching it and firing your rocket in the air.

2 Launch it!

You can launch the rocket right away if you're not interested in stabilizing and decorating it. To do this, tie the two ends of one piece of clothing elastic into a knot. Hold the knot in one hand and point the rocket at the sky. Hook the other end of the elastic into the notch in the rocket. Pull back on the rocket as far as you dare and release.

Tip: It might be wise to wear thin gloves the first few times you launch your rocket, or until you get the hang of it. Eventually you will develop the technique of not firing the rocket into your fingers! Otherwise, attach the elastic to the end of a strong piece of cardboard and use that instead, like so:

3 Add strength

If you want to make the rocket fly further and straighter, add weight to the head end. Draw around the tip of your rocket on another piece of cardboard. Stop about 2½ in. (6 cm) down the body of the rocket. Do the same again and cut out both pieces of cardboard. Cut a V shape into the end of each piece and glue one to each side of the rocket head.

4 Add stability

Add extra fins at the base to stabilize the rocket. These should match the size and shape of the fins on the rocket base. The easiest way to do this is to lay your rocket on the cardboard, draw around the base, and cut it out. Then cut a slot into the body of the main rocket exactly down the middle and exactly the width of the cardboard the fins are made of, as shown below. Glue the fins into the slots and wait for the glue to dry.

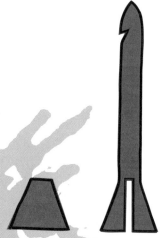

5 Decorate it

White paint is a good choice for a rocket, because it can then be "rocketized" with black paint, aluminum foil, markers, and glitter.

Variation:

Experiment with different shapes. Try wider fins and firing the rockets horizontally to see if they will glide. You could even try making the world's first flying shark.

How to play the game:

You can use the rockets for a target game. Stack some boxes on top of each other, with the open ends facing you. Place the bigger ones at the bottom and the smaller ones on top and give them each a score. Aim the rockets into the boxes from far away. If you throw them like javelins, rather than firing them with the elastic, you may find it improves your aim.

Indoor Den

This is a custom-built den and secret meeting place. Instead of extending your house on the outside you extend it inside, filling your room with what appears to the untrained eye to be just a whole pile of empty cardboard boxes.

Time: You can spend as long on this as you like, but half a day will give you a good den.

Parental stress factor: ❹ This is potentially high due to the fact that our indoor den is very big and parents never like big.

Fiddly bits: None.

You will need

- several really big cardboard boxes
- scissors or craft knife
- masking, duct, and/or packing tape

1 Grasp the basic idea

You just tape several big boxes together, cutting door spaces out of the cardboard as you go so that you can move from one box to another. You can make the arrangement as simple or complicated as you like.

Tip: A good alternative if you have lots of space is to make a huge tunnel to crawl through, with turns and twists like a maze. A big box placed at the end of the tunnel makes an excellent HQ.

Dinosaurs

These are realistic 3-D dinosaurs (well, as realistic as cardboard dinosaurs can ever be). As dinosaurs are extinct, there are no conservation issues so they can also make great subjects for target practice.

Time: About an hour per dinosaur.
Parental stress factor: ❶ This could go up depending on who is using the craft knife.
Fiddly bits: Cutting the shapes requires a sharp craft knife. No doubt your parents will insist they have the steadier hands. Let them have their way, but supervise parents with sharp implements at all times so that they can't blame you if they cut themselves.

You will need

- pencil
- craft knife
- sheet of thick cardboard, about 14 in. x 12 in. (36 cm x 30 cm) per dinosaur
- assorted paints and paintbrush

Tip: Use cardboard that is about ⅛ in. (3 mm) thick. Thicker than this and it will be difficult to cut out; thinner than this and it will not be strong enough.

1 Copy the template and cut out your creature

Choose your dinosaur and copy the template onto a piece of cardboard following the method given on page 8. Carefully cut out the body and the legs with a craft knife.

2 Paint your dinosaur

Decorate your dinosaur however you want. Because no one has ever seen a living dinosaur, you can use glitter and glow-in-the-dark paint and still claim to be biologically accurate. Paint one side of the body and legs and let it dry. Turn it over and paint the other side. When the paint is dry, slot the front and back legs into the body.

Variation:

If you like making these figures, you might consider making one on a much larger scale. Use the same procedure, but make your dino as big as you like. After you've cut it out, use it as a pattern to draw a second one and glue the two pieces together. This will make it stronger. It will look very impressive guarding your bedroom and could become a useful place to put clothes that haven't quite made it back to the dresser.

Tyrannosaurus Rex

Literally the "Tyrant Lizard," this massive meat-eating giant had powerful jaws lined with teeth 6 in. (15 cm) long. It could probably run quite fast and would certainly bring tears to your eyes if it kicked you!

The Cardboard Box Book

Apatosaurus

The "Thunder Lizard" spent much of its time submerged in water to help support its enormous weight of approximately 27 tons. It was so big that it had to spend most of its time eating just to stay alive!

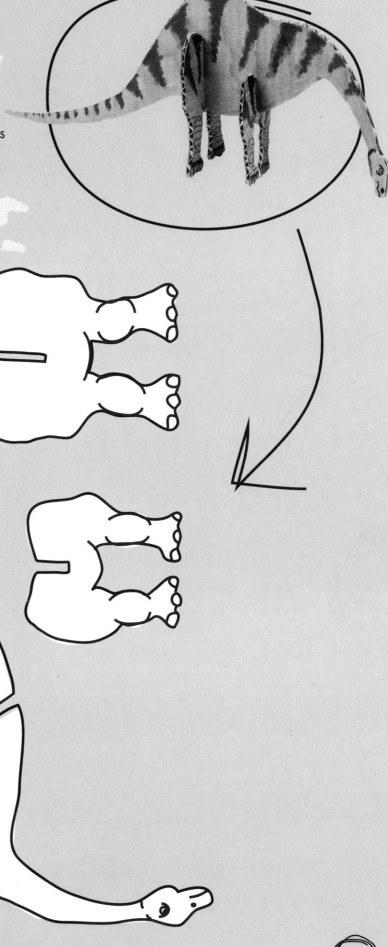

Styracosaurus

The "Spiked Lizard" was not to be messed with. At around 16½ feet (5 meters) long it must have looked pretty scary with its horns around its head and neck.

Stegosaurus

A slow but deadly vegetarian, this dinosaur had bony plates along its back and sharp spikes at the end of its tail. To make the rear legs of this dinosaur, cut out the front legs and then draw a slightly larger outline around them to make the back legs.

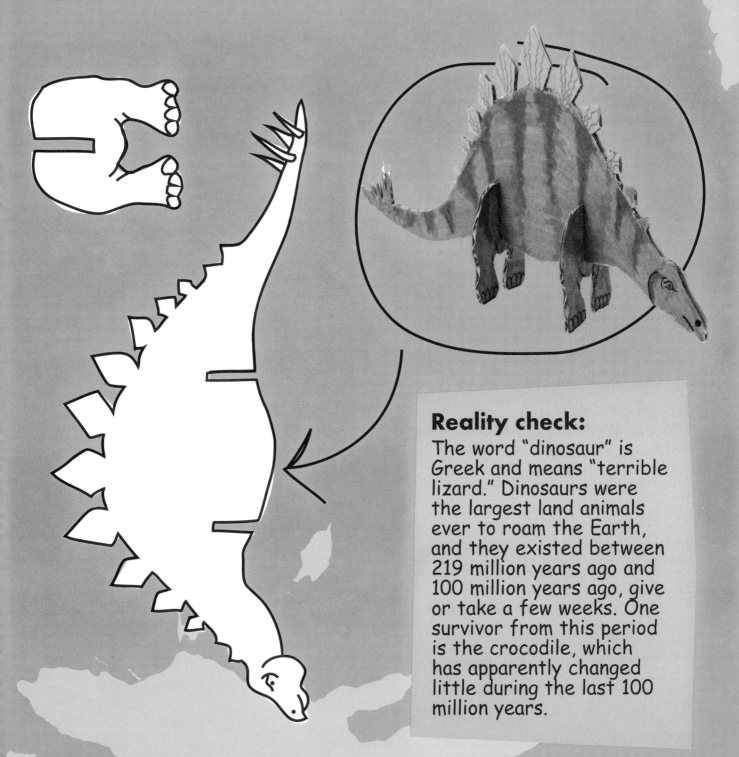

Reality check:

The word "dinosaur" is Greek and means "terrible lizard." Dinosaurs were the largest land animals ever to roam the Earth, and they existed between 219 million years ago and 100 million years ago, give or take a few weeks. One survivor from this period is the crocodile, which has apparently changed little during the last 100 million years.

Fishing Game

This classic game has been around for years. Played with fishing rods, magnets, and fish with paperclips in their mouths, it is great fun and totally unpredictable.

Time: Allow a couple of hours to decorate the box, make the fishing rods, and make and decorate the fish.

Parental stress factor: ❶ There's nothing here to upset them unless, of course, you insist on inspecting their fishing permits when they ask to play.

Fiddly bits: Cutting out the fish shapes neatly is the only slightly fiddly part.

You will need

- scissors or craft knife
- medium-sized cardboard box
- assorted paints and paintbrush
- pencil
- PVA glue and small brush
- paperclips
- glitter (optional)
- black marker
- 2 pieces of string, about 20 in. (50 cm) long
- 2 pieces of garden stake, bamboo, or sticks, about 2 feet (60 cm) long
- 2 magnets

1 Paint the box

Cut the top off the box and keep the pieces of cardboard to make the fish. Decorate the outside with a watery design. We chose to paint a wave, the seabed, a blue sky, and some fish, but feel free to make a more realistic scene with shopping carts on the seabed and floating soda bottles on an oil-polluted surface if you wish.

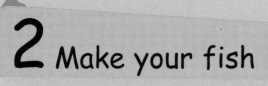

Make your fish

While the paint dries, draw some fish on the spare cardboard using the fishy templates to the right. (See page 8 for instructions on making templates.) Cut them out and glue a paperclip to the mouth of each one. Paint or decorate the fish in some way—glittery fish look good. When the paint has dried, use the marker to write a score of one or two on the back of each fish. This gives each person a reasonable chance to win.

3 Assemble the rods

Tie a piece of string to one end of each stick, piece of bamboo, or garden stake, then glue or tie a magnet to the loose end of the string and you are ready to play.

How to play the game:
• Each person dangles his or her fishing rod into the box without looking in and tries to "hook" a fish. Take turns fishing until all the fish are caught. Add up the numbers on the individual fish, and the person with the highest number wins.

• Extend the game by making more and smaller fish, as well as booby prizes such as shopping carts and old boots that are, of course, worth no points. You can also glue paperclips to the screw tops of soda bottles and other small items of junk.

• Don't forget to make a sign saying, "Private Fishing."

The Cardboard Box Book

Road Layout

This massive road scheme is a project that can be done pretty quickly or developed over time.

Time: This depends upon how big you want it to be and on the number of features you want to add. You can spend days on a full cityscape, half an hour on a large layout without much detail, or somewhere in between for a moderately detailed plan.

Parental stress factor: ❶ The road layout folds flat so it can be stored underneath a bed, sofa, or the dog, hidden behind a cupboard, or buried in the garden.

Fiddly bits: None, unless you design a really elaborate version (highly recommended!).

You will need

- scissors or a craft knife
- 2 sheets of thick cardboard, about 5 feet x 18 in. (1.5 meters x 46 cm)
- wide masking tape
- paper
- pencil
- black marker
- assorted paints and paintbrush or color felt-tip pens
- magazine pictures, computer labels, aluminum foil, etc., for decoration (optional)
- additional thick cardboard (optional)

Tip: Make sure the roads are wide enough for your cars and that the blocks of land are big enough to fit a grocery store, hospital, or whatever. And be sure to include plenty of parking spaces.

1 Make your base

Place two long sides of the cardboard sheets side by side and tape them together all the way along the join with plenty of wide masking tape. Turn over the cardboard and you have your naked surface ready to be transformed. Because you have taped it down the center, your base can be folded and put away when you have finished.

2 Get creative

Get a blank sheet of paper and design your road layout. Because the cardboard base is taped down the middle, it is best to have a road running all the way along the join. You can expand your town from there. First draw the roads, railroad tracks, and river then add blocks of land. To the right is a rough drawing of how ours first looked.

3 Transfer your design onto the board

Use a black marker to transfer your plan to the cardboard. If you only have half an hour to spend on the project, get your cars out for a spin now.

4 Embellish it a little bit

If you have a little more time, color the grassy areas in green, the river in blue, the buildings in brown or gray, the fire station in red, etc. We would recommend leaving the roads unpainted: just use a black marker to put in lines and road markings. Now you're done. Go cruising!

5 Embellish it a lot

If you have lots more time, go all out for this magnificent version, recommended by readers of *Cardboard City Weekly*. Cut out large blocks of land shapes from other bits of cardboard, paint them green, and stick them onto the baseboard in the positions on your plan. You will now have a 3-D patchwork of roads and fields like so.

6 Add buildings

If you're making the elaborate, eight-day version of this project, now it is time to cut out cardboard shapes for all the buildings in your plan. Maybe stick in a few burger restaurants, a swimming pool or bowling alley, and don't forget the library or movie theater. Color these with paint or felt-tip pens so that they stand out and stick them into place. Now you have a 3-D surface with added strength.

Variations:

If you have more time than sense (like we do), here are some more ideas to try:

• Draw in the railroad tracks, road markings, and parking spaces.

• Print out computer labels for all the major sites, such as the fire station and supermarket, and stick these onto the buildings.

• Browse through magazines and cut out shop logos, pictures of fire engines, police cars, etc., and stick these onto the relevant buildings.

• Make a large park by sticking down aluminum foil for a lake, adding twigs and stones, and drawing trees, bushes, and paths.

• Add a church with a graveyard. This is not strictly necessary, but will satisfy your morbid curiosity and sense of the grim reality of life.

• If you're really clever (and we would award you The Cardboard Box Book Gold Medal for this if you pull it off), light up the whole thing with lightbulbs (as described on page 9). Street lighting!

Christmas Diorama

The diorama shows the scene of a room at Christmas viewed through a front window and illuminated from within by simple lights. It looks very festive in the evening as Christmas draws near.

Time: The diorama can be made in a few hours, though obviously if you take more care and spend more time, it will look even better.

Parental stress factor: ❶ This might just help get you that special present!

Fiddly bits: Some expertise with sticky tape and nimble scissor work is required. Fixing up the lighting also might be a little tricky.

You will need

- pencil and ruler
- scissors or craft knife
- medium-sized cardboard box
- craft glue
- masking tape
- assorted Christmas wrapping paper
- spare pieces of cardboard
- old Christmas cards
- Christmas decorations, such as streamers and baubles
- matchboxes
- assorted paints and paintbrush
- clear acetate
- 2 small pieces of fabric

For the lighting (see page 9)

- 1 battery holder
- 2 1.5-volt batteries (AA size)
- 2 bulb holders
- 2 2.5-volt bulbs with screw fittings
- small switch
- insulating wire

1 Start with the window

Cut a hole in one end of your box leaving about 1 in. (2.5 cm) all around. Glue and tape down the flaps in the floor and roof of the box so that you have something like this:

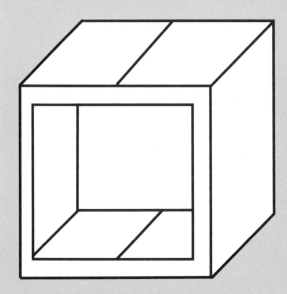

2 Decorate the box

Now cover the outside of the box in Christmas wrapping paper. The easiest way to do this is to cut squares or rectangles the size of the floor, walls, and roof and stick them down with glue. Cover the inside of the box in the same way. For the inside choose something with a small pattern so that it looks like wallpaper.

3 Design the room

Select old Christmas cards that have pictures of fireplaces with roaring fires, an open door with carol singers, windows looking out at snowy scenes, presents, Christmas trees, small pictures to hang on the wall, and a Father Christmas figure, preferably with a sack of presents. Add these to the room. If you can't find all of these things, draw them on cardboard and color them in or try some of the suggestions given on the following pages.

4 Assemble the room

Add your pictures to the room, looking through the front to make sure you are happy with their positions. Glue some to the walls, making a few stick out into the middle of the box. Some can be placed in the middle of the room by taping a thick bit of cardboard at the back to prop them up, like so:

Tip: Cut a Christmas tree shape out of thick cardboard. Paint it green and the pot red. Decorate the tree with blobs of colored paint to look like lights and add some glitter. String some tinsel around it, and stick on sequins to look like baubles.

5 Add some glitz

Raid your parents' Christmas wrapping and decorations box for a few more 3-D elements. Those fancy bows that people stick on presents to cover up the mess they made wrapping them are useful. Use a couple as wall decorations. Hang some tiny baubles from the ceiling and add shiny ribbons that look like streamers. Cover matchboxes with wrapping paper, tie a ribbon around them, and place them beneath the tree as presents.

Tip: Other shapes you can make are a lantern, some holly, and a tree surrounded by gifts. You can also print out pictures with a Christmas theme from Clip Art on your computer. Color them in and glue them to cardboard.

6 Make a window

Cut a piece of cardboard the same size as the open end of the box. Paint this end piece black. When the paint has dried, cut a hole in it, leaving a wide border all around so that it covers the 1 in. (2.5 cm) lip. Glue a piece of clear acetate onto the back of the window hole. Next cut out a piece of cardboard a little larger than your window hole and cut four smaller windows in it just like the drawing to the right. Paint it a lighter color so that it contrasts with the black of the front wall. When it is dry, glue it over the window hole.

7 Add curtains

For that finishing touch, cut two pieces of fabric and stick them to the back of the window to look like curtains.

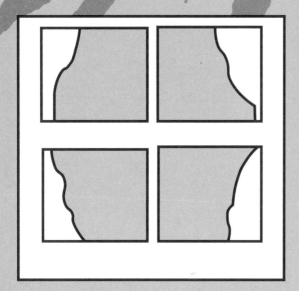

8 Fit your window

Stick the window frame to the front of the box so that it covers the big hole. Tape it along the top so that it hinges and can be left open or closed. This window adds to the charm and gives it a "wow" factor, as it makes you feel like you are looking into a real room.

9 Light it up!

The lights are what make this diorama so impressive. Study the interior of your box carefully and use a flashlight to decide where to place your bulbs for maximum effect. You might want a light in front of the scene if it is dark, or you may wish to place one behind Father Christmas or a tree, thus creating some very effective back lighting. Cut holes on both sides of the box big enough to push bulbs through and wire them up according to Jake's excellent wiring diagram and instructions on page 9.

Variations:

Your diorama doesn't have to stick to a Christmas theme. Here are some other ideas.

Winter Wonderland Diorama

Make the scene in the box a picture of the outside world: snowy and cold, with skaters carrying parcels, and trees covered in ice. Recycle old Christmas cards for this. Spray some artificial snow on everything, artistically of course. This will look stunning when illuminated.

Farm Diorama

Re-create a farm scene with buildings and animal pens made from cardboard (what else), and add lots of toy animals, tractors, etc. Paint the walls to look like the sky and fields. Make it more realistic by adding bits of moss, leaves, and straw. Throw in some manure to achieve a greater sense of realism.

Jungle Diorama

Use twigs and fresh leaves, with green string for vines. Add monkeys, snakes, parrots, and any other small jungle toys you may have. Squashed raisins make great elephant droppings.

Halloween Diorama

Make it ghoulish with ghosts, goblins, witches, headless horsemen, bats, pumpkins! Dream up your own spooky illumination.

Garden Diorama

Replicate your garden in 3-D.

Outer Space Diorama

Make a moonscape with craters, a spaceship, and astronauts, or reproduce the planetary system with some eerie lighting.

Climbing Wall

The climbing wall is a replica mountainside that your action figures can climb up. It can also form the backdrop for a mission base.

Time: About an hour plus glue- and paint-drying time.
Parental stress factor: ❶ This should cause no parental alarm.
Fiddly bits: None.

You will need

- scissors or craft knife
- large cardboard box
- pencil
- craft glue
- black, white, and green paint and paintbrush

Tip: The bigger the cardboard box you can find, the higher your mountain will be!

1 Cut out the shape

Cut out one side of the box and draw the outline of your mountain on it. Make sure you allow enough cardboard for a base as well as the wall itself. When you are happy with the shape, cut along the pencil line with the craft knife. You will then have something that looks like this:

2 Add some rocks

Cut out some largish, irregular pieces from the rest of the box. Glue these onto the mountain to begin making it 3-D, like so:

3 Build up layers

Add a second layer of smaller "rocks" on top of the larger ones with pieces of cardboard in the same way, like this:

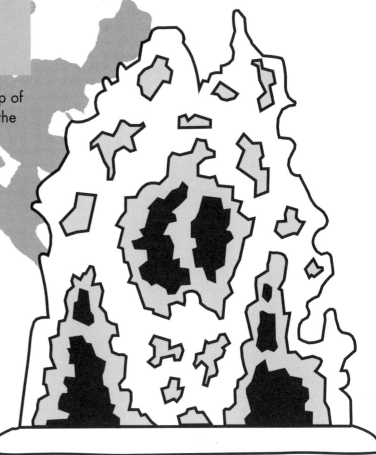

4 Cut out holes

When all the glue has dried, cut a few holes through the cardboard here and there to add more hand- and footholds for your action figure to cling to.

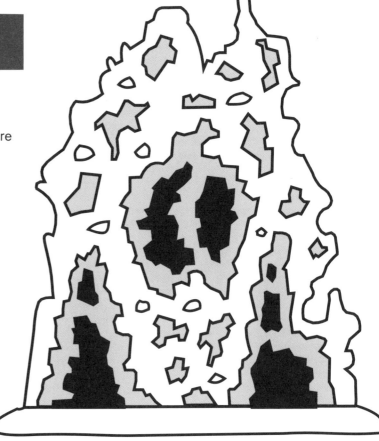

5 Paint your mountain

The mountain is now ready for use, but to add that extra bit of realism paint it various shades of gray with specks of green here and there to represent rocks and lichen. Lean your mountain up against a real wall, to keep it sturdy and avoid nasty climbing accidents.

Play House

For this project you need the kind of huge box that comes free with a freezer or washing machine—big enough that you can get in and out of it easily.

Time: The basic house can be thrown together quite quickly, but you could spend days adding to it. Take your time and decorate it gradually.

Parental stress factor: ❸ The scale of this project could cause high parental blood pressure. You are likely to lose your allowance if you include a garage and a conservatory. (Don't even mention the swimming pool.) On the other hand, if you disappear into it for hours at a time you should earn some points.

Fiddly bits: The basic house is not difficult to make, just BIG. However, if you insist on adding central heating and a jacuzzi . . .

You will need

- huge cardboard box
- wide masking tape
- pencil and ruler
- scissors or craft knife
- 1 small box for the chimney
- craft glue
- cardboard tube
- clear acetate or saran
- assorted paint and paintbrush
- 1 small box for the shelves
- fabric
- big-eyed needle and thread
- string
- 2 fruit boxes (optional)

1 Build the roof

Fold the two longest flaps into a peak and join them together with plenty of strong tape. Fold up the two short flaps and, with a pencil, trace a line where they meet the sloped roof. Cut off the four corners from the short ends and tape the ends securely to the roof. You may also want to strengthen the base of your cardboard box with more tape.

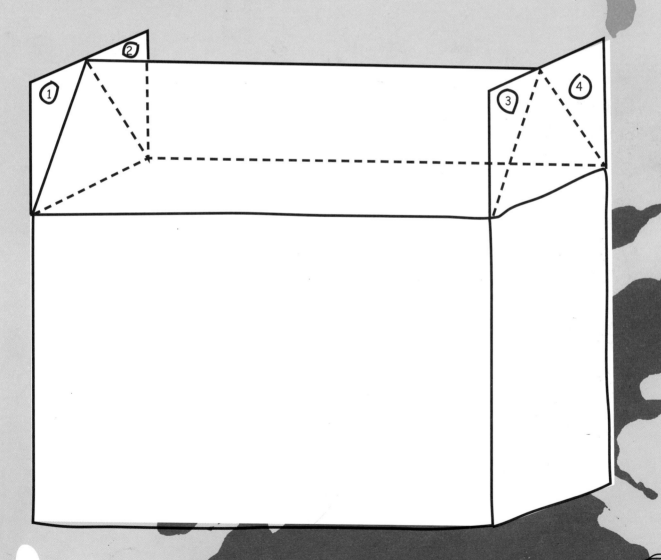

2 Add the chimney

Take a small box and cut out a V shape to match the angle of your roof. Slot the box in place and secure it to the roof with lots of tape. Cut a piece off of the cardboard tube and glue it to the box.

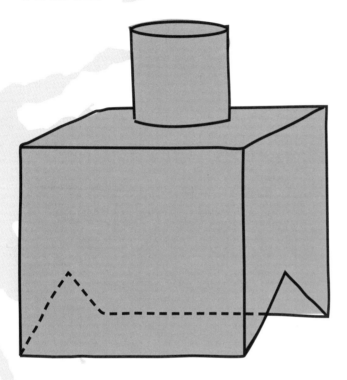

3 Make doors and windows

Use your pencil and ruler to mark the position of a door. Cut out three sides with the craft knife. Score the fourth side and leave as a door hinge. Score and cut out the windows and tape the acetate or saran over the inside of each one.

4 Decorate your house

Paint the outside walls and the roof any color you like. We painted our roof brown and added tiles to it. We gave the door a doorknob and a knocker, and added a house number. Use the flower templates below to decorate the outside of your house. (See page 8 for full instructions on working with templates.) You might decide to go for the haunted house look, or prefer a log cabin. You may want to paint the inside as well.

Tip: Every house should have a treasure chest, also known as a shoebox. Decorate the box and use it to store your personal stash of goodies: candy, bottles of cola, rare comics for use as bargaining tools, pictures of your dog, bits of string, etc.

5 Add shelves

You will need plenty of these inside the house for storing essentials such as a flashlight and chocolate, and on the outside for holding stuff like windowboxes. Make the shelves by cutting the corners off another box. You can also use fruit boxes to create the frames for your shelves, as we did.

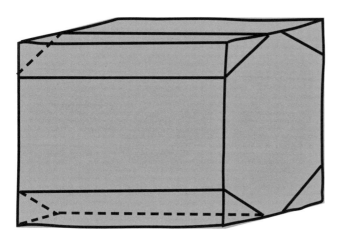

6 Create curtains

To guarantee privacy in your play house, hang up some curtains. Cut the fabric for each curtain to about one-and-a-half times the width of the window, and hem it along the top. Thread the string through the hem. Inside the house, make two holes on either side of the window. Pass the ends of the string through the cardboard to the outside of the house with a big-eyed needle. Pull both ends tight and tie them with a large knot. You can now open and close your curtains whenever you like. You can also add lighting. (See page 9 for instructions.)

Variations:

• Make a general store, post office, or junk shop. (The parental stress factor can easily be reduced if you sell something, providing it isn't theirs.)

• Open a café and serve lemonade to your friends.

Insect Box and Bug Catcher

At last, here is a box in which to keep insects while you examine and identify them, before releasing them back into the dining room. This super deluxe, "dual view" box comes complete with instructions for your very own bug catcher.

Time: Both the box and the bug catcher can be made in an hour.

Parental stress factor: ❹ This all depends upon whether your parents like ants, spiders, and other small, hairy life forms. In order to test the likely parental response, cup your hands and bring them up close to your mother's face, while at the same time saying, "Mom, do you like spiders?" Note the response and proceed accordingly.

Fiddly bits: None. The hardest part is making a hole in the jar lid. We suggest you let a parent do that part.

You will need

- shoe box
- pencil and ruler
- scissors or craft knife
- clear acetate
- masking tape
- twigs and leaves
- 2 pieces clear plastic tubing, each ½ in. (1 cm) wide, 1 piece about 8 in. (20 cm) long, the other about 14 in. (35 cm) long (available from automotive stores)
- plastic jar with plastic, screw-top lid
- drill or bradawl
- sandpaper
- muslin or nylon stockings
- magnifying glass (optional)

1 Make the windows

With the pencil and ruler, mark a border around the front of the shoe box about 2 in. (5 cm) from the edge. Cut along the line to make a hole in the box front. Do the same to the lid of the shoe box so you end up with a box that has a window in the front and one on top.

Reality check:

A bug catcher is an essential piece of the naturalist's equipment. Danny first came across one in a forgotten corner of the old school biology lab, alongside many other cobweb-covered Victorian devices.

2 Secure the acetate with tape

Tape acetate to the insides of these windows to keep your critters from escaping. You should end up with something like this:

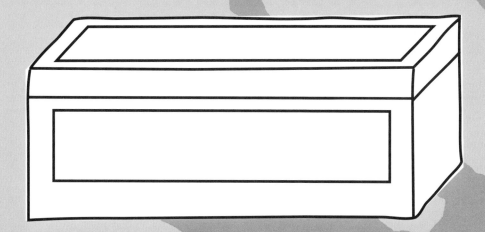

3 Add some twigs

Before filling your box with creatures, put in some twigs and leaves so that the insects have something to eat while serving their time. Don't put in too many leaves though, or you will not be able to see your specimens. It should look something like this:

4 Make holes for the bug catcher

Ask an adult to make two holes in the top of the plastic jar lid with a drill or a bradawl. The two pieces of plastic tubing have to fit through the holes, but be held tight. To get this right, ask your adult to make the holes small, then you can gradually sand them bigger with some sandpaper wrapped around the tip of a pencil.

5 Add the tubing

Place both lengths of tubing through the jar lid. Wrap a bit of very thin material around the end of the shorter tube. (This will be the sucking tube.) Use a piece of muslin or your mother's best nylon stockings. Tape the fabric tightly to the tube, as this will prevent you from sucking the insects down into your lungs. The bug catcher should look something like this, only better.

6 Go hunting

A good place to look for small forms of wildlife is in that pile of socks and underpants under your bed. However, if you are unusually clean and tidy, head out to the garden or your local park.

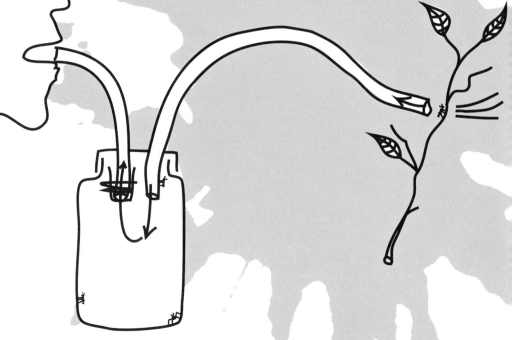

7 Collect a bunch of insects

Get down low and look at ground level. Rummaging among dead leaves usually turns up some tasty morsels. Direct the tube close to the target and take in a sharp breath, sucking up the insect. Make sure the sucking-tube cover is in place or you might just get an unwanted snack.

8 Gather some leaves

Collect a piece of the plant you found the insects on for your box, as it is likely that this will be their food plant.

9 Show your critters around their new home

When you have collected enough insects, unscrew the jar lid and gently tip them into the box, along with the plant material you collected. If you have a magnifying glass, use it to try to identify your creatures.

10 Show off!

Get a good book and learn a few Latin names, then ask your father if he'd like to inspect your collection of "Coleoptera" and "Diptera." Ask him if he can spot the "Crawlalongus Twiglettium."

Wall Window

This is a mock window for a bare wall that can act as a photo frame, poster, notice board, or just a piece of art.

Time: The basic window frame can be completed in an hour, but decorating it with the collage will take longer.

Parental stress factor: ❶ All the horrors of the other projects will be forgotten if you include your parents' photographs. Clever, eh!

Fiddly bits: Some cutting and some messy glue stuff.

You will need

- scissors or craft knife
- large cardboard box
- pencil and ruler
- PVA glue and small brush
- magazines, postcards, and photos
- assorted paint and paintbrush
- felt-tip pens (optional)
- big-eyed needle or small screwdriver
- string
- glitter, sequins, ferns, grasses, etc. (optional)

1 Make the frame

Cut out the two biggest sides of your box. One side will be the base board. On the other side, draw a window following the pattern to the right Cut out the inner panes, but hang on to the cardboard for later.

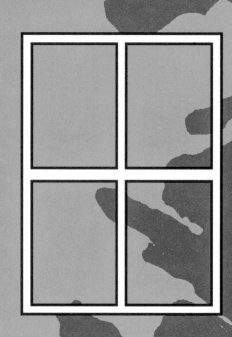

2 Create a collage

Place the window frame over the base board and draw around the inside of the squares so that you end up with four window shapes. Remove the frame and glue images from magazines, postcards, and photos onto the windows. This is where artistic license and personal taste can run free. We made a collage of sky and scenery, but you should re-create whatever you'd like to see when you look out of your window: the ocean, a football stadium, a snowy mountainside, whatever.

3 Color the frame

Decide where you are going to hang the finished window and color the frame appropriately. Paint the frame and let it dry. You will add more decoration later, but it is best to get the background color on before you glue the frame over the collage.

4 Poke some holes

Make four holes with a big-eyed needle or the end of a small screwdriver at the points shown in the base board. Take a piece of string and tie a large knot at one end. Thread it from the back through one of the lower holes, then through the hole above, then across the back and through the top hole on the opposite side. Thread it through the lower hole out to the back of the window again. Pull it tight and tie another large knot and cut off any excess string. Here is a diagram of the route as taken by the actual piece of string we used:

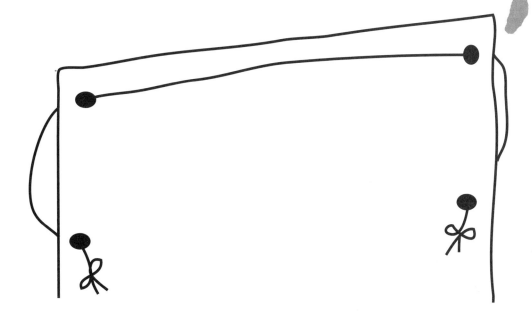

5 Glue it together

Turn over the frame, spread plenty of glue around the edges, and carefully place it over the collage. Place weights such as heavy books on the frame and let it dry.

6 Decorate the frame

Now jazz up the frame a bit. You can use glitter and sequins to give it a special Barbie-type effect. Or if you have painted the frame a manly brown, you could add ferns and grasses to it, giving it more of an outdoor feel.

7 Add windowsills

Remember in Step 1 we told you not to chuck out the bits from the middle of the window? That's because they are exactly the width of the windows, so cut strips 1 in. (2.5 mm) wide and glue them to the base of each window pane. Now you have four little windowsills for . . . stuff!

Tip: Smaller versions of the wall window make great picture frames and are ideal gifts.

Space Rocket

Prepare for take off! You are now going to build a rocket. This project is one of our favorites because the possibilities are endless.

Time: This is a biggie that could keep you occupied for at least a week or two.
Parental stress factor: ❹ This depends on how big it ends up and how long you sit in it saying, "Houston, we have a problem," and "That's one small step for a man, but . . ."
Fiddly bits: Not many, although the retro injector warp drive can be tricky.

You will need

- 1 enormous box
- 3 more boxes approximately half to a third of the size of the big one
- extra sheet of cardboard a little smaller than one large side of the big box
- tape measure
- wide masking tape
- pencil and ruler
- scissors and craft knife
- 1 fruit box
- black and colored markers
- old bits of electronic equipment, such as switches, wires, and funny-looking diode thingies
- clear acetate or saran
- assorted paints and paintbrush
- aluminum foil
- 4 cardboard tubes
- PVA glue and small brush

For the lighting (see page 9)

- 1 battery holder
- 2 1.5-volt batteries (AA size)
- 2 bulb holders
- 2 2.5-volt bulbs with screw fittings
- small switch
- insulating wire

1 Assess the hangar capacity

Lay the four boxes together on the ground, side by side, and measure the overall length. If you plan to stand the rocket upright when it's finished and it's longer than the height of your room, find some smaller boxes.

2 Prepare your main capsule

Draw and then cut a large U shape on the longest side of the box for the door. Score the uncut side of the door to make a hinge. You should make sure you can get in and out (but only just). A large door weakens the hull and is likely to break up on re-entry. Make a porthole so you can see what's going on in the outside world. Just cut a hole in the right-hand wall somewhere and tape a sheet of acetate or saran over it. Finally, cut a hole the exact size of your second-largest box in the top of the first box. You'll find out why in Step 6.

3 Add a shelf

You will need a shelf for your lasers, rations, transmitters, spare underpants, whatever. The wall facing you as you enter the capsule is a good place for one. Cut the fruit box in half lengthwise and fix it securely to the wall with plenty of tape.

4 Rig up some lights

The easiest way to add light is to use a flashlight, but it's a lot more fun to have working lights inside. Tape a battery holder for 2 1.5-volt batteries (with the batteries in, of course) onto the extra sheet of cardboard and rig up a couple of bulbs in bulb holders. Wire up a switch along the way, then tape all these in place and you will have a dim but very cosy cabin. Jake's circuit diagram (below) will illuminate (sorry!) the process.

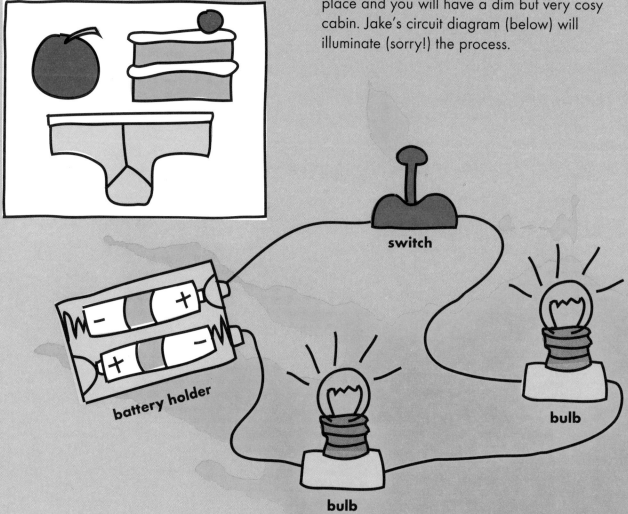

switch

battery holder

bulb

bulb

Tip: An onboard CD or MP3 player is essential for your sanity on long flights. Perhaps not as essential as chocolate, but a close second.

5 Take control

We can't give exact instructions here, but you need to draw or tape most or all of the following onto your sheet of cardboard: lots of dials, buttons, switches, force-field energizers, reverse-thrust booster levers, alien detectors, warp-factor analyzers, and a manual override for the automated navigation system. Then you will have a control panel that you should tape securely to the left-hand wall of your main capsule as you enter.

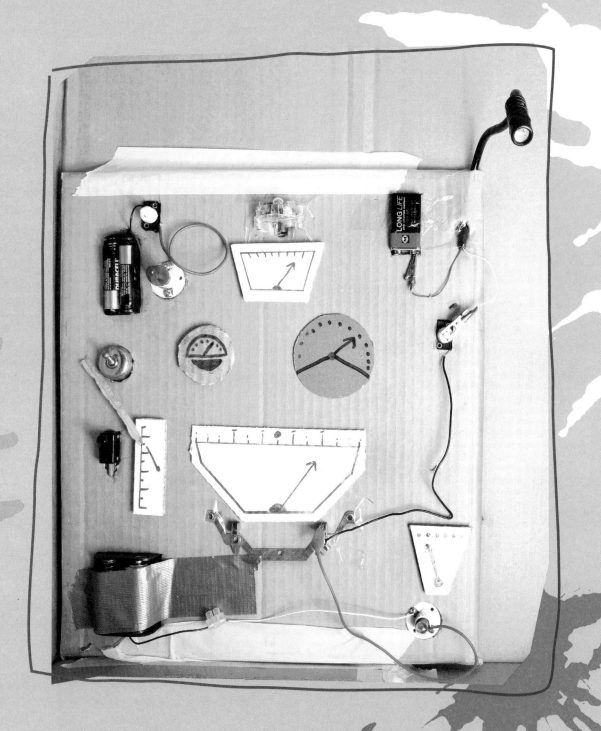

6 Add an escape hatch

Open one end of your second-largest box and pull out the flaps. Place the box over the hole in the top of the capsule, then cut the flaps flush to the outside edges of your largest box—you don't want them to get caught on anything as you hurtle through space! Tape the two boxes together. You will probably have to rest the capsule on its side to do this. From the outside, cut out a door in one side of the second-largest box for your escape hatch.

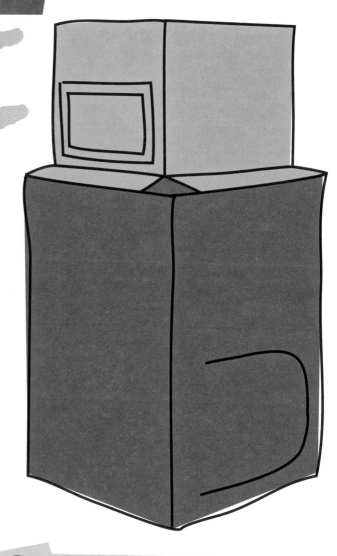

7 Finish it off

Add another box on top of the second one for added height. To make the pointed top of the rocket, take your final box and cut it diagonally in half. Tape this to the top of the other three boxes. Now you're almost ready for takeoff!

8 Decorate it

Nothing withstands the enormous temperatures generated upon re-entry as well as heat resistant ceramic tiles, but paint is a lot cheaper and lighter. When the paint is dry, draw in the lines of the body panels, rivets, and any logos you want with markers. Glue on aluminum foil to look like platinum-reinforced panels. Add rocket propellors—cardboard tubes painted silver—to each of the corners of the main capsule. Get some rations, grab your space suit, climb in, and set the coordinates for the planet Zog.

The Cardboard Box Book

Guessing Box

Ask friends and relatives to put their hands in the box (if they dare) and try to guess what's lurking inside. It is not advisable to use highly venomous snakes.

Time: A rough but ready-to-use version can be made in under half an hour. Allow about an hour if you wish to decorate the box.
Parental stress factor: ❷ This depends on what you put in the box.
Fiddly bits: None.

You will need

- shoe box, preferably with a hinged lid
- masking tape
- felt-tip pens
- piece of thick fabric
- scissors or a craft knife
- range of differently shaped objects

1 Make a lid and cut a hand hole

If your box doesn't have a hinged lid, tape one long side of the lid to the box with plenty of tape. In one short end of the box, cut a hole just large enough to put your hand through.

2 Decorate the box

Cover the box sides and lid with question marks or any pattern that strikes your fancy.

3 Cover it up

Cut a piece of thick fabric that is long enough to drape over the inside and the outside of the end of the box with the hole in it. Tape the fabric over the top edge of the box so it hangs down on both sides of the hand hole.

4 Have fun!

Place lots of things in the box—chunks of jello, a banana that is starting to rot, a dead fish, and your pet rat spring to mind—and invite people to put their hands through the hole and guess what's inside.